MW01687462

# geography now

## Student Workbook

# geography now

## Student Workbook


**SENIOR AUTHOR**
Graham Draper

**AUTHORS**
Wayne Andrew
Bert Duncan
Angie Roth



THOMSON
NELSON

Australia Canada Mexico Singapore Spain United Kingdom United States

THOMSON
NELSON

*Geography Now* Student Workbook

**Senior Author**
Graham Draper

**Authors**
Wayne Andrew
Bert Duncan
Angie Roth

**Director of Publishing and Customer Solutions**
Beverley Buxton

**General Manager, Social Studies, Business Studies, and Languages**
Carol Stokes

**Publisher, Social Studies and Business Studies**
Doug Panasis

**Executive Managing Editor, Special Projects**
Cheryl Turner

**Managing Editor, Development**
Karin Fediw

**Product Manager, Social Studies and Business**
Nadia McIlveen

**Program Manager**
Norma Pettit

**Developmental Editor**
Isobel Stevenson

**Editorial Assistant**
Natalie Russell

**Executive Director, Content and Media Production**
Renate McCloy

**Director, Content and Media Production**
Lisa Dimson

**Content Production Editor**
Joyce Funamoto

**Copy Editor**
Geraldine Kikuta

**Proofreader**
Linda Szostak

**Production Manager**
Cathy Deak

**Production Coordinator**
Susan Ure

**Design Director**
Ken Phipps

**Cover Design**
Johanna Liburd

**Cover Image**
© John Foster/Masterfile

**Compositor**
Brenda Prangley

**Photo/Permissions Researcher**
Paula Joiner

**Printer**
Courier Kendallville

**REVIEWERS**
The authors and publisher gratefully acknowledge the contributions of the following educators:

Ian Brimble
York Catholic District School Board

Lou Iaccino
York Region District School Board

Rachelle Y. Séguin
Limestone District School Board

**Aboriginal Content Reviewer**
Brenda Davis
Six Nations of the Grand River Territory



ISBN-13: 978-0-17-630230-6

ISBN-10: 0-17-630230-1

Printed and bound in the United States Of America

1 2 3 4 10 09 08 07

For more information contact Nelson, 1120 Birchmount Road, Toronto, Ontario, M1K 5G4. Or you can visit our Internet site at http://www.nelson.com

# Table of Contents

# Introduction

## I.1 Looking Inside *Geography Now*

# I.1 Looking Inside *Geography Now*

**How I Am Being Assessed** ______________________________

______________________________

You will need your student book, *Geography Now*, and your *Geography Now Student Workbook* to complete this activity.

1. How many chapters are there in *Geography Now*? ______________________

2. What is the number of the chapter with the title "The First People in Canada"? ____

3. What is the title of the fourth unit in *Geography Now*? ______________________

   ______________________________

   ______________________________

4. *Geography Now* has some special features to help you study geography. Write down the number of a page on which there is an example of each feature:

   Key Words ______
   Literacy Skill ______
   Case Study ______
   GeoTechnology ______
   GeoCareers ______
   FASTFact ______
   Literacy Strategy ______

5. What is the topic of the Unit 1 Performance Task in your *Geography Now Student Workbook*? ______________________

   ______________________________

   ______________________________

6. What is the purpose of the Appendix on pages 258 to 268 of *Geography Now*?

   ______________________________

   ______________________________

   ______________________________

7. On what page of the Glossary will you find the definition for *system*? ________

8. Go to the Index on pages 276 to 281 of *Geography Now*. Which pages in the book refer to the topic of ecozones? ______________________________

9. On what pages of the workbook are the activities for Chapter 9, People Patterns?

______________________________________________

10. Give the number of one workbook activity that contains a map of Canada.

______________________________________________

# Unit 1 PHYSICAL SYSTEMS

# 1.1 Physical and Human Systems Involved in Buying a Donut

**How I Am Being Assessed** ______________________________

______________________________________________

1. a) **Figure 1.6** on page 8 of *Geography Now* gives details about the physical and human systems involved when someone buys a television. Complete this chart about the physical and human systems involved when you buy a donut.

| Processes | Physical Systems Involved | Human Systems Involved |
|---|---|---|
| **Manufacturing:** Making the donuts | | |
| **Marketing:** Making customers want to buy the donuts | | |
| **Transportation:** Shipping the raw materials and the finished donuts | | |
| **Sales:** Selling the donuts to the customers | | |
| **Service:** Helping the customers to enjoy their donuts | | |

Figure 1: Physical and Human Systems Involved in Buying a Donut

b) In what ways are a television and a donut the same?

______________________________________________

______________________________________________

c) In what ways are a television and a donut different?

______________________________________________

______________________________________________

2. The cartoon in **Figure 2** below is the same as the one in **Figure 1.1** on page 2 of *Geography Now*. Here the words spoken have been deleted. Make up three new statements that could be written in the speech balloon. Your new statements should be humorous and should show what you know about systems.

Figure 2: System Cartoon

Statement 1: ______________________________________________

______________________________________________

______________________________________________

Statement 2: ______________________________________________

______________________________________________

______________________________________________

Statement 3: ______________________________________________

______________________________________________

______________________________________________

# 2.1 Forces Building the Land

**How I Am Being Assessed** ______________________________

______________________________

1. Write the key words from Chapter 2 in *Geography Now* in the space below:

______________________________

______________________________

______________________________

______________________________

2. Rewrite the list of key words, beginning with the word that you find the easiest and ending with the word that you find the most difficult. Next to each word, write the reason you ranked it as easy or difficult. Your reasons could include that the word is easy to spell, difficult to pronounce, a familiar word, and so on.

| **Words in Order of Difficulty** | **Reason for Ranking of Word** |
|---|---|
| | |
| | |
| | |
| | |
| | |
| | |

3. Write the specific geographical term that each of the following clues refers to on the line next to the clue. (To help you, we have given you the page number on which you can find each term in *Geography Now*.)

   1. Oldest landform region in Canada (2 words) (p. 18)

   ______________________________

 

2. Flow of energy inside the earth (2 words) (p. 15)

______________________________________________

3. Means "mountain," found in Western Canada (p. 12)

______________________________________________

4. Time from the formation of the earth to present day (2 words) (p. 17)

______________________________________________

5. Formed globally by heat from the earth's core (p. 14) ____________________

6. Existed around 135 million years ago (p. 14) ____________________

7. Hudson Bay ______________________ landform region (p. 12)

8. Melted rock that filled the Sudbury Basin (p. 15) ____________________

9. Second most recent era (p. 18) ____________________

10. Was 10 km wide and formed the Sudbury Basin (p. 15)

______________________________________________

11. Second oldest era (p. 18) ____________________

12. Means "all lands"; existed 200 million years ago (p. 14)

______________________________________________

13. Large slabs of rock that make up the earth's crust (p. 12)

______________________________________________

14. The study of the movement of large crustal slabs (2 words) (p. 12)

______________________________________________

15. Oldest era of geologic time (p. 18) ____________________

16. Has different characteristics than other places (p. 13)

______________________________________________

17. Area where there are many earthquakes and volcanoes (3 words) (p. 16)

______________________________________________

18. Scientist who studies seismic waves (earthquakes) (p. 17)

_______________________________________________

19. Where one plate slides below another (2 words) (p. 15)

_______________________________________________

20. Mining centre sits in huge crater formed by meteorite (p. 15)

_______________________________________________

4. Find all the terms you identified in question 3 in the following word puzzle.

| | | | | | | | | | | | | | | | | | | | |
|---|---|---|---|---|---|---|---|---|---|---|---|---|---|---|---|---|---|---|---|
| B | H | T | O | Q | A | R | V | V | X | X | S | M | A | G | M | A | S | T | R |
| E | O | S | M | T | X | S | C | I | N | O | T | C | E | T | E | T | A | L | P |
| J | N | X | V | Z | Y | D | L | C | H | R | E | O | T | S | N | H | D | D | W |
| I | X | L | M | A | P | A | N | F | R | G | L | R | I | E | O | Y | Z | Y | Y |
| N | S | U | D | B | U | R | Y | K | E | O | S | Q | R | I | Z | Z | O | C | J |
| V | A | C | E | R | I | F | F | O | G | N | I | R | O | S | N | E | O | D | Y |
| J | Y | N | A | Z | A | B | D | I | I | H | U | V | E | M | O | T | A | I | D |
| A | F | S | Z | N | A | E | C | O | O | C | K | T | T | O | I | C | O | J | C |
| I | I | K | R | A | A | T | S | S | N | P | A | O | E | L | T | L | I | H | X |
| A | R | E | L | L | I | D | R | O | C | L | H | M | M | O | C | R | A | I | Q |
| J | X | B | H | M | N | A | I | I | P | G | H | Z | Y | G | U | T | G | F | J |
| G | P | X | E | A | N | T | O | A | S | U | T | H | U | I | D | L | I | K | J |
| K | K | E | L | Y | C | Z | D | E | N | Y | Q | U | O | S | B | O | Z | V | D |
| V | D | W | M | E | O | K | N | G | Z | S | Z | N | O | T | U | A | T | E | G |
| I | O | T | V | E | O | A | Q | N | L | U | H | P | H | I | S | R | Q | J | Y |
| L | X | N | L | P | R | E | C | A | M | B | R | I | A | N | C | P | S | A | M |
| C | O | A | S | C | G | C | Y | P | Z | Y | B | E | E | Z | D | G | O | R | V |
| C | P | V | T | S | I | X | X | G | Z | F | I | D | Z | L | N | S | E | T | J |
| B | N | V | L | A | D | T | R | P | C | B | I | Z | V | K | D | B | X | H | S |
| P | Y | D | G | I | K | J | D | Q | R | B | V | O | J | C | U | N | Z | V | Z |

5. Fill in the blanks in the sentences below:

a) ______________________ is the total time from the formation of the earth to the present day.

b) Continental plates are very thick and move around at the rate a ____________ grows.

c) The ________________________________ is said to be a hotbed of seismic activity.

d) The ________________________________ Mountains are found in the Arctic region of Canada.

e) The ____________________ Mountains are found on the east coast, while the ______________________________ is found on the west coast of Canada.

f) The flow of energy inside the earth creates ________________________ These, in turn, cause the earth's crustal plates to move around.

g) The ____________________________ era is the oldest in geologic time.

h) ________________________________ are places where one plate slides below another.

i) The oldest rocks in the Canadian Shield are __________________________ ______________________ old.

j) ________________________________ has had an important role in creating mountains, shields, and plains in Canada and the rest of the world.

## 2.2 Mapping

**How I Am Being Assessed** ______________________________

______________________________

1. a) Mark Canada's landform regions on the map below, using the information supplied in **Figure 2.2** on page 13 of *Geography Now*.

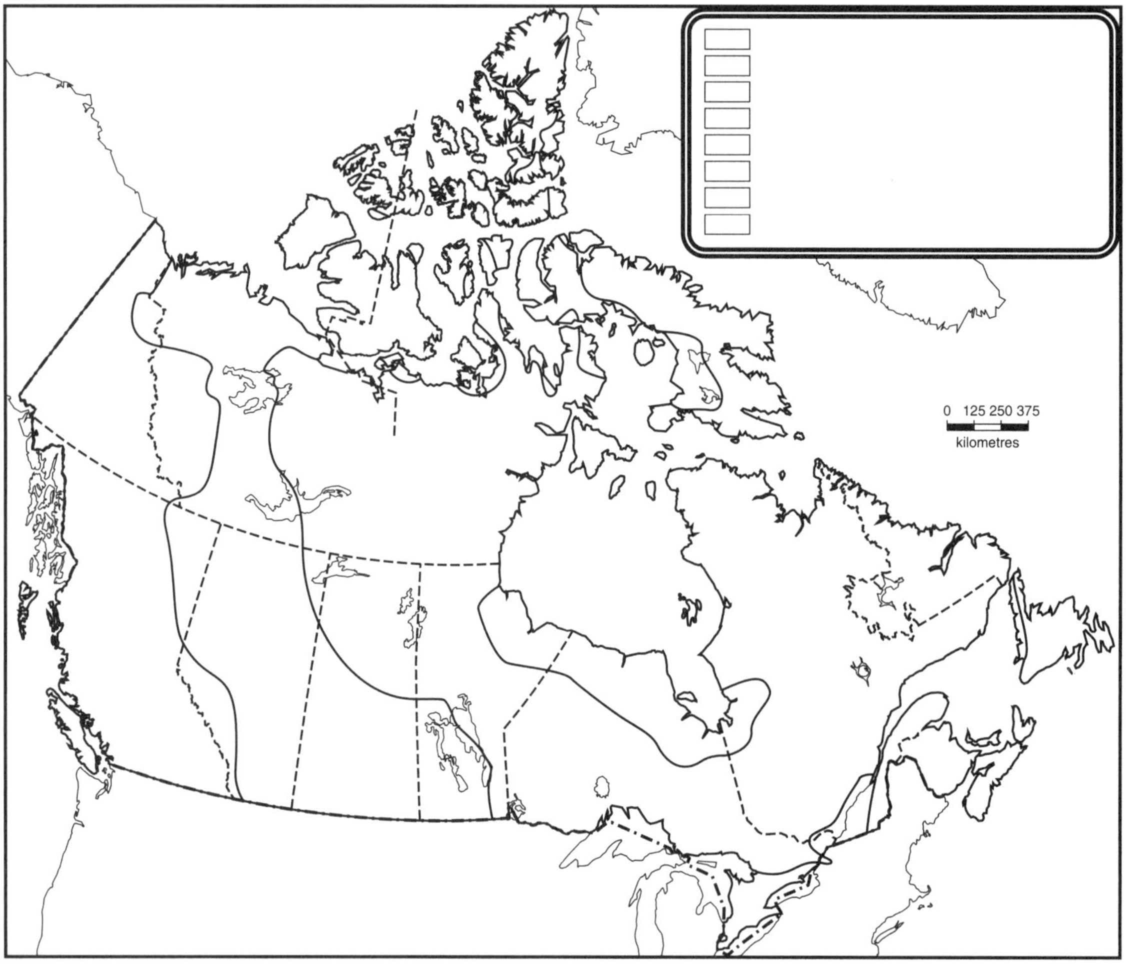


Figure 1: ______________________________

b) Give your map a title and a legend.

| | | | |
|---|---|---|---|
| | | | |
| | | | |
| | | | |
| | | | |

c) Put an arrow on your map to indicate which direction is north.

2. The names of geographic regions are based on different characteristics, including
   - geographic location (Arctic, Hudson Bay, Great Lakes)
   - physical features (plains, mountains, shield)
   - direction (north, south, east, west)

Suggest how each of the landform regions listed in **Figure 2** below was named. There may be more than one answer. The first region has been filled in for you.

| **Region** | **How It Was Named** |
|---|---|
| **Western Cordillera** | Western – direction; Cordillera – physical feature |
| **Interior Plains** | |
| **Innuitian Mountains** | |
| **Hudson Bay Lowlands** | |
| **Canadian Shield** | |
| **Appalachian Mountains** | |
| **Great Lakes–St. Lawrence Lowlands** | |
| **Arctic Lowlands** | |

Figure 2: Derivation of Names of Landform Regions

3. What pattern can you see in the way landform regions are named?

# 3.1 The Water Cycle

**How I Am Being Assessed** ______________________________

______________________________

1. a) How many millions of cubic metres of water move through the water cycle each day? To find the answer, fill in the right-hand column in **Figure 1** below, using the information given in **Figure 3.2** on page 22 of *Geography Now*, and then add up the numbers in the column.

| Form of Water | Cubic Metres of Water per Day (in Millions) |
| --- | --- |
| Infiltration and percolation | |
| Streamflow to oceans | |
| Total surface and groundwater flow to oceans | |
| Evaporation and transpiration from surface water bodies, etc. | |
| Atmospheric moisture | |
| Precipitation | |
| Human use | |
| Total amount of water moving through the water cycle each day | |

Figure 1: Amount of Water Involved in the Water Cycle Each Day

b) Which form of water has the greatest volume in the water cycle?

______________________________

______________________________

c) Which forms of water have the least volume in the water cycle?

______________________________

______________________________

______________________________

2. Imagine you are a single drop of water. Write a letter explaining your journey through the water cycle. Be sure to explain where you encounter the largest amount of water in your journey.

## 3.2 Shaping the Land

**How I Am Being Assessed** ____________________

____________________

1. a) Fill in the middle column of **Figure 1**, stating what you think each term in the first column means.

| Term | What I Think It Means | Definition in *Geography Now* |
|---|---|---|
| glaciation | | |
| glaciers | | |
| zone of accumulation | | |
| zone of ablation | | |
| deposition | | |
| Columbia Icefield | | |
| hydrologic cycle | | |
| water cycle | | |

 

| Term | What I Think It Means | Definition in *Geography Now* |
|---|---|---|
| weathering | | |
| erosion | | |

Figure 1: Key Terms

b) Now read Chapter 3 in *Geography Now*, and then use the information there and in the Glossary to complete the right-hand column in **Figure 1**. How do your original definitions compare with those in *Geography Now*?

2. Put an X in the appropriate column in **Figure 2** to indicate whether each word in the left-hand column is related to the work of water or the work of ice. If it is related to both, put an X in both columns.

| | Work of Water | Work of Ice |
|---|---|---|
| weathering | | |
| glaciation | | |
| moraine | | |
| evaporation | | |
| moisture | | |
| erosion | | |
| till | | |
| deposition | | |
| hydrologic cycle | | |
| solar radiation | | |
| crevasses | | |
| transpiration | | |
| drumlin | | |
| kettle lakes | | |
| clouds | | |

Figure 2: The Work of Water and Ice

## 3.3 Chapter Review Test

**How I Am Being Assessed** ______________________________

______________________________

1. Indicate whether each of the following statements is true or false. Use the page number (indicated in brackets) to help you decide.

   a) The water cycle and hydrologic cycle both refer to the same thing. (p. 22) T F

   b) The Rocky Mountains are much older than the Appalachians. (p. 20) T F

   c) In chemical weathering, water dissolves some chemicals found in rock. (p. 21) T F

   d) Erosion involves movement, while weathering does not. (p. 21) T F

   e) Glaciers flow from the zone of ablation to the zone of accumulation. (p. 23) T F

   f) Melt water flows away from the glacier snout, carrying debris with it. (p. 23) T F

   g) Sand, gravel, and clay are examples of material deposited by glaciers. (p. 24) T F

2. Explain how glaciers created good farmland. Use the words *till*, *glacier*, *melt water*, and *deposition* in your answer.

______________________________

______________________________

______________________________

3. Why do the peaks on the Rocky Mountains look more jagged than the peaks in the Appalachians?

______________________________

______________________________

______________________________

______________________________

4. What does the term *glacial till* mean?

______________________________________________

______________________________________________

5. Match the definitions in the column on the left to the words in the column on the right.

| | |
|---|---|
| ___ where snow is melting on a glacier | A. glaciation |
| ___ breaks rocks into pieces | B. hydrologic cycle |
| ___ when water carries away weathered rock | C. Columbia Icefield |
| ___ occurs when snow freezes | D. weathering |
| ___ created when more snow falls than is melted | E. zone of ablation |
| ___ water cycle | F. glaciers |
| ___ where snow is added on a glacier | G. erosion |
| ___ located on boundaries of Banff and Jasper National Parks | H. zone of accumulation |

6. Fill in the blanks in the following sentences:

a) The difference between weathering and erosion is that erosion involves ____________________ while weathering does not.

b) Wind, ________________, and gravity are responsible for wearing away the surface of the land.

c) Weathering breaks rocks into pieces in two ways: ________________ and ____________________.

d) Chemical erosion is when water ______________ some of the chemicals found in rocks.

e) Glaciers have two distinct zones: the ____________________ and the ____________________.

# 4.1 Climate and Weather

**How I Am Being Assessed** ______________________________

______________________________________________

1. Write a definition for each of the terms in **Figure 1** below:

| Term | Definition |
|---|---|
| weather | |
| climate | |
| latitude | |
| air mass | |
| relief precipitation | |

Figure 1: Important Definitions

2. a) If climate were the main consideration, would you prefer to stay in Victoria, Iqaluit, Toronto, or St. John's? To help you answer the question, fill in the table in **Figure 2**, using the information provided in **Figure 4.1 (a–c)** on page 28 of *Geography Now*.

| | January Temperature (°C) | July Temperature (°C) | Annual Rainfall (mm) |
|---|---|---|---|
| **Victoria** | | | |
| **Iqaluit** | | | |
| **Toronto** | | | |
| **St. John's** | | | |

Figure 2: Climate Characteristics of Some Canadian Cities

b) I would prefer to stay in ______________________________

because ______________________________

______________________________

______________________________

______________________________

3. Using the climate data below and the grid marked in **Figure 3**, create a climate graph for London, Ontario, similar to the one shown in **Figure 4.2(a)** on page 29 of *Geography Now*.

| **London, ON** | **Jan** | **Feb** | **Mar** | **Apr** | **May** | **Jun** | **Jul** | **Aug** | **Sep** | **Oct** | **Nov** | **Dec** |
|---|---|---|---|---|---|---|---|---|---|---|---|---|
| **Daily Average (°C)** | -6.3 | -5.5 | -0.3 | 6.3 | 13.0 | 18.0 | 20.5 | 19.5 | 15.3 | 9.0 | 3.1 | -3.0 |
| **Daily Maximum (°C)** | -2.4 | -1.4 | 4.2 | 11.6 | 19.0 | 23.8 | 26.3 | 25.2 | 20.9 | 14.0 | 6.9 | 0.6 |
| **Daily Minimum (°C)** | -10.1 | -9.7 | -4.7 | 1.0 | 7.0 | 12.1 | 14.6 | 13.7 | 9.6 | 4.0 | -0.7 | -6.5 |
| **Precipitation (mm)** | 74.2 | 60.0 | 78.4 | 82.2 | 82.9 | 86.8 | 82.2 | 85.3 | 97.7 | 77.6 | 91.1 | 88.6 |

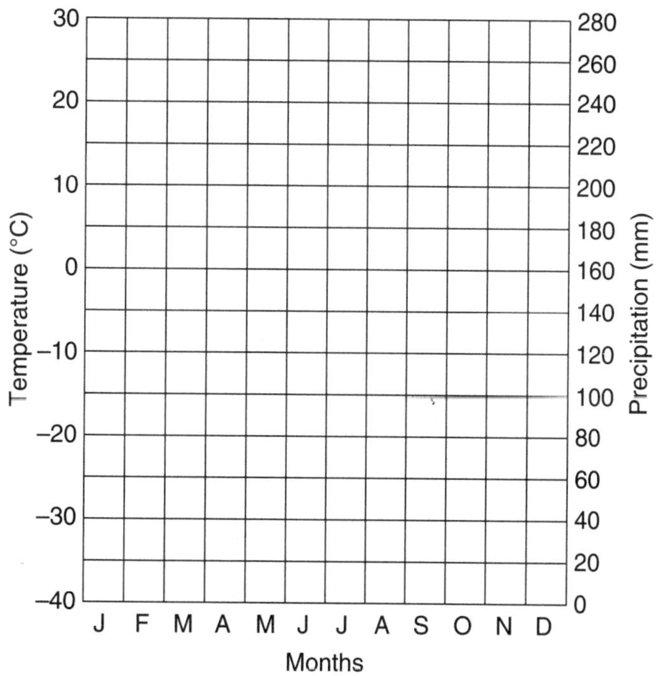


Figure 3: Climate Graph for London, Ontario

4. Using the climate data below and the circle marked in **Figure 4**, create a circular graph of the climate in Edmonton, Alberta, similar to the one shown in **Figure 4.2(b)** on page 30 of *Geography Now*.

| Edmonton, AB | Jan | Feb | Mar | Apr | May | Jun | Jul | Aug | Sep | Oct | Nov | Dec |
|---|---|---|---|---|---|---|---|---|---|---|---|---|
| Daily Average (°C) | -13.5 | -10.5 | -4.5 | 4.3 | 10.4 | 14.1 | 15.9 | 15.1 | 10.1 | 4.3 | -5.7 | -11.3 |
| Precipitation (mm) | 22.7 | 13.0 | 16.0 | 26.3 | 49.9 | 87.4 | 95.2 | 70.3 | 47.1 | 19.8 | 17.7 | 17.3 |

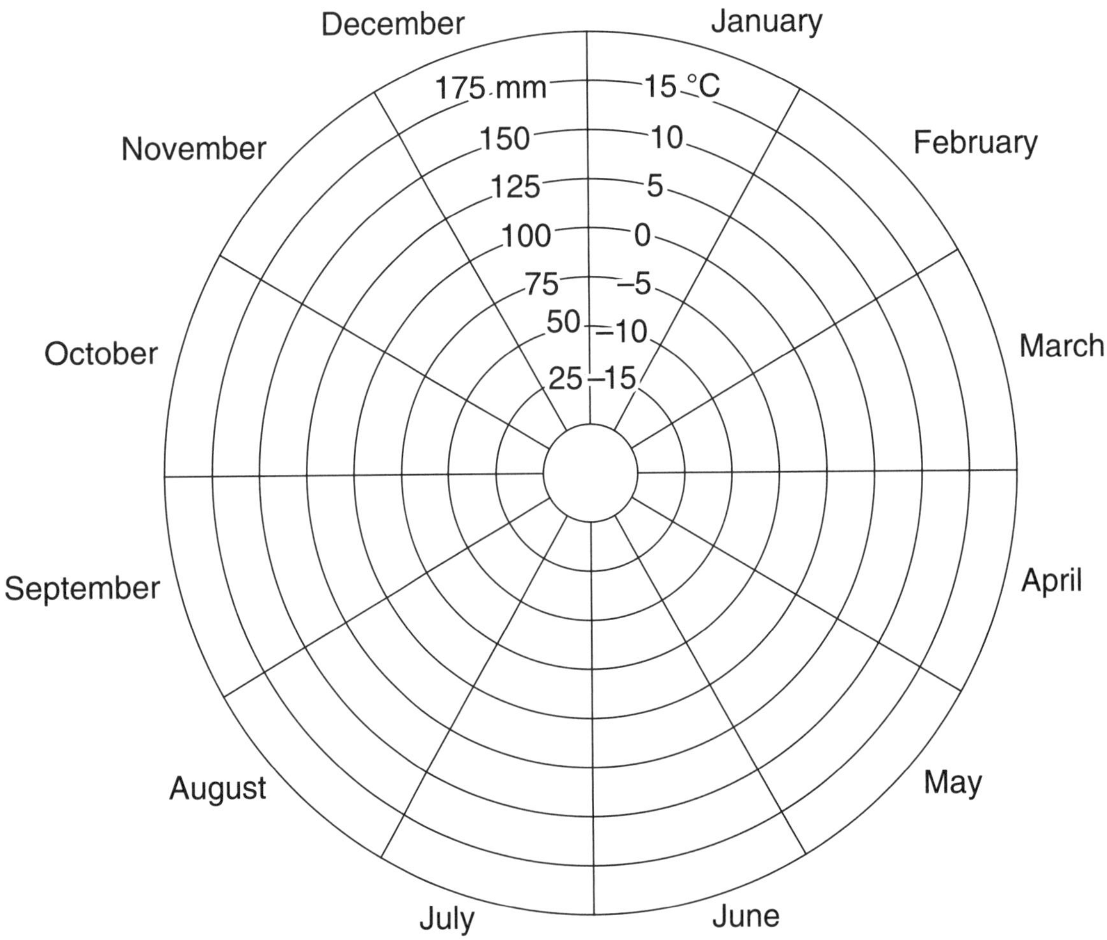


Figure 4: Circular Graph of the Climate in Edmonton, Alberta.

 

5. a) Using the climate data below and the grid marked in **Figure 5**, create a hythergraph for Windsor and Yellowknife, similar to the one shown in **Figure 4.2(c)** on page 30 of *Geography Now*.

| **Windsor, ON** | **Jan** | **Feb** | **Mar** | **Apr** | **May** | **Jun** | **Jul** | **Aug** | **Sep** | **Oct** | **Nov** | **Dec** |
|---|---|---|---|---|---|---|---|---|---|---|---|---|
| **Daily Average (°C)** | -4.5 | -3.2 | 2 | 8.2 | 14.9 | 20.1 | 22.7 | 21.6 | 17.4 | 11 | 4.6 | -1.5 |
| **Precipitation (mm)** | 57.6 | 57.3 | 75 | 85.1 | 80.8 | 89.8 | 81.8 | 79.7 | 96.2 | 64.9 | 75.5 | 74.7 |

| **Yellowknife, NWT** | **Jan** | **Feb** | **Mar** | **Apr** | **May** | **Jun** | **Jul** | **Aug** | **Sep** | **Oct** | **Nov** | **Dec** |
|---|---|---|---|---|---|---|---|---|---|---|---|---|
| **Daily Average (°C)** | -26.8 | -23.4 | -17.3 | -5.3 | 5.6 | 13.5 | 16.8 | 14.2 | 7.1 | -1.7 | -13.8 | -23.7 |
| **Precipitation (mm)** | 14.1 | 12.9 | 13.4 | 10.8 | 19.1 | 26.9 | 35 | 40.9 | 32.9 | 35 | 23.5 | 16.3 |

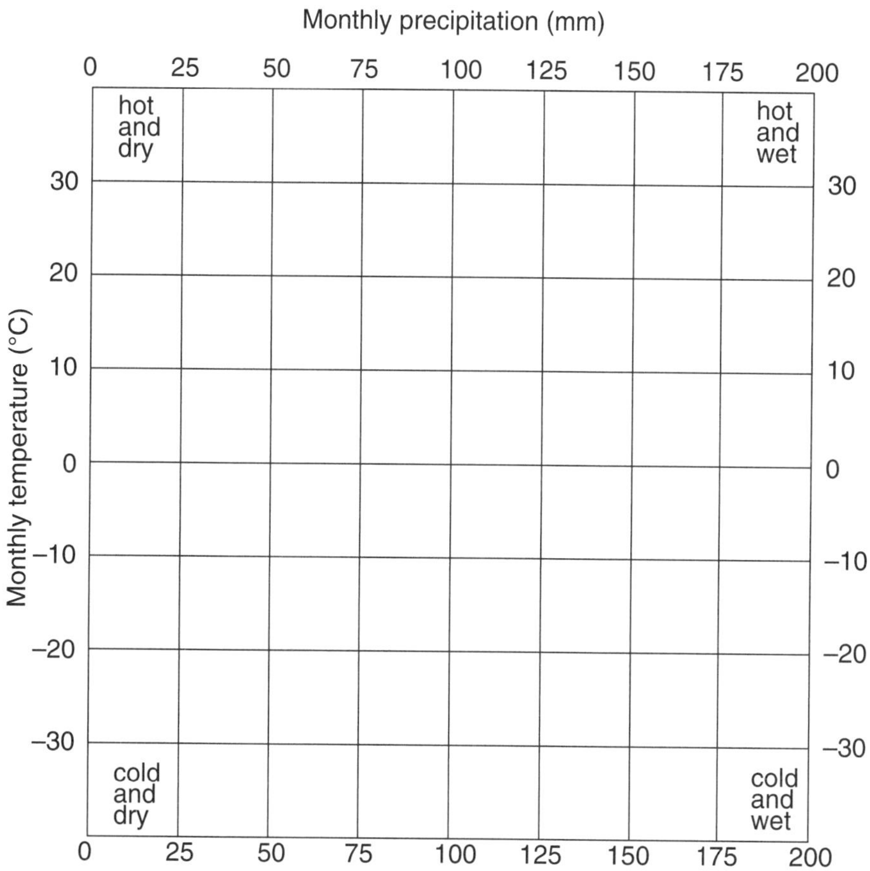


Figure 5: Hythergraph of Climate Data for Windsor and Yellowknife

b) Look at the graphs you have drawn. Why is it easier to compare the climates of Windsor and Yellowknife than those of London and Edmonton?

# 4.2 Climate Cartoons

**How I Am Being Assessed** ______________________________

______________________________________________

1. Provide as many possible punch lines as you can for the cartoon below. Here are some questions to get you started:
   - What are the people in the picture doing?
   - What does their clothing tell you about the weather/climate?
   - What do their facial expressions tell you about what they are thinking?
   - Who is speaking to whom?
   - What first comes to mind when you look at the cartoon? Does someone in the photo know something important?

www.CartoonStock.com

Figure 1

______________________________________________

______________________________________________

______________________________________________

______________________________________________

# 4.3 Climate Scavenger Hunt and Review

**How I Am Being Assessed** ______________________________

______________________________

1. a) The six factors that influence climate are found on page ______ .

   b) What acronym can you use to remember these factors? ______________

   c) List the three global factors that affect climate:

      i. ______________________________

      ii. ______________________________

      iii. ______________________________

   d) Why are these called *global* climate factors?

   ______________________________

   ______________________________

2. a) In this chapter, the Case Study is found on page ______ .

   b) List five key facts about the 1998 ice storm.

      i. ______________________________

      ______________________________

      ii. ______________________________

      ______________________________

      iii. ______________________________

      ______________________________

      iv. ______________________________

      ______________________________

      v. ______________________________

      ______________________________

3. a) On which page are the guidelines for reading graphs?_______

b) What are the five key steps to remember when reading graphs?

i. ____________________

ii. ____________________

iii. ____________________

iv. ____________________

v. ____________________

4. a) The Geocareer featured in the chapter is____________________

b) What type of education does a meteorologist need to have?

____________________

____________________

5. Write a short paragraph explaining how human beings affect climate change.

____________________

____________________

____________________

____________________

____________________

____________________

____________________

6. What is the topic of the FASTFact in this chapter?

____________________

____________________

____________________

____________________

7. **Using the Internet**. Brainstorm a list of Hollywood movies that show the power of severe weather or climate change. Then use the Internet to research two movies and summarize what each of them says about weather or climate.

______________________________________________

______________________________________________

Movie Title #1: ______________________

Summary

______________________________________________

______________________________________________

______________________________________________

______________________________________________

______________________________________________

______________________________________________

Movie Title #2: ______________________

Summary

______________________________________________

______________________________________________

______________________________________________

______________________________________________

______________________________________________

______________________________________________

## 5.1 Natural Vegetation Regions

**How I Am Being Assessed** ______________________________

______________________________________________

1. Research each of the natural vegetation regions in Canada and summarize your findings in the chart in **Figure 1**.

| Region | Coniferous Forest | Deciduous Forest | Temperate Rain Forest | Prairie | Tundra |
|---|---|---|---|---|---|
| Word Description | | | | | |
| Example Species | | | | | |
| Sketch or Photograph | | | | | |

Figure 1: Natural Vegetation Regions of Canada

# 5.2 Permafrost in Canada

**How I Am Being Assessed** ______________________________________

______________________________________________________________

1. Shade the four permafrost regions of Canada on the map in **Figure 1** below. Use the same colours to shade the legend.

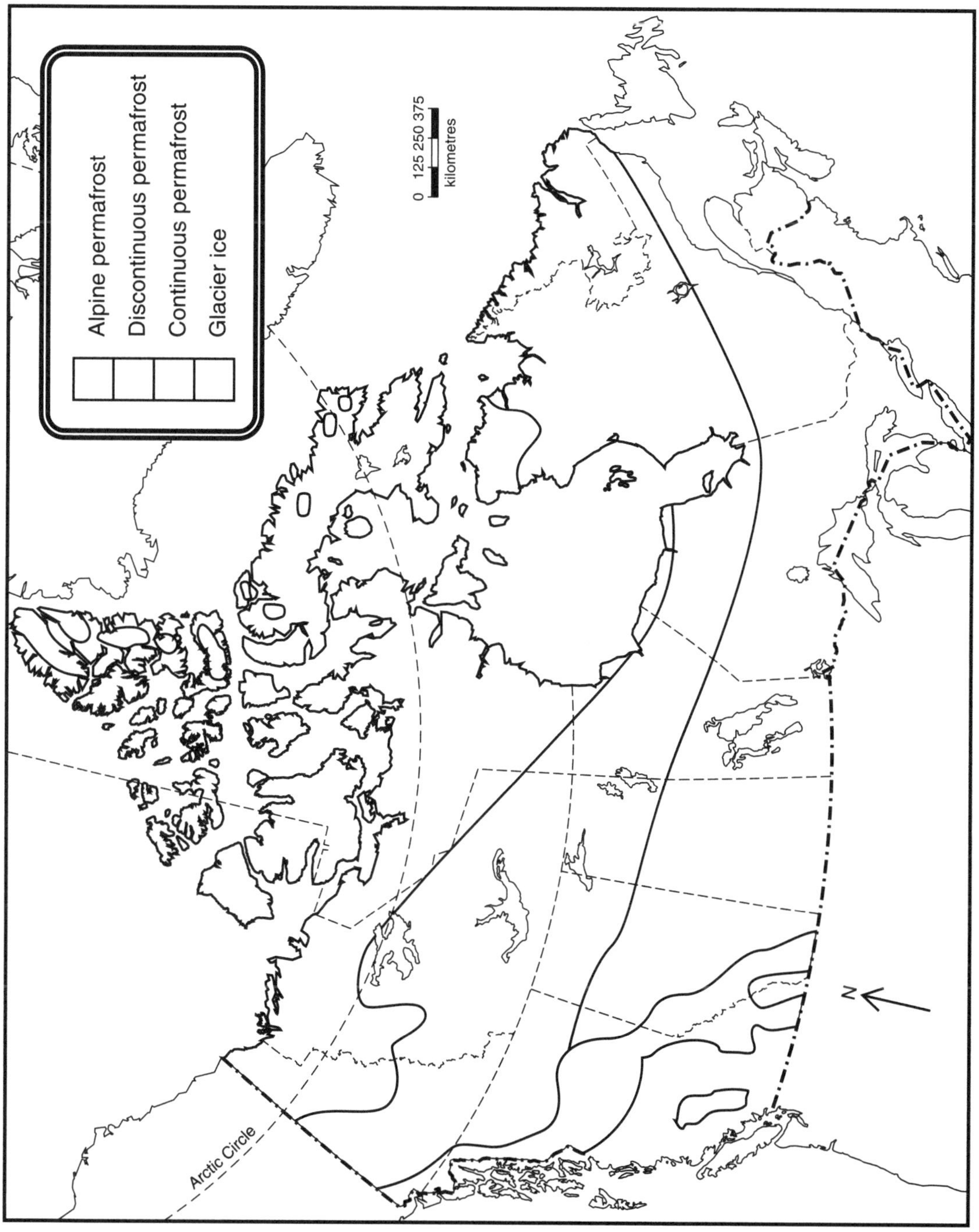


Figure 1: Permafrost Regions in Canada

2. a) Label and colour the cross-section (side-view) diagram in **Figure 2** to show the three zones of permafrost. The attached legend should help you work out where the labels should go.

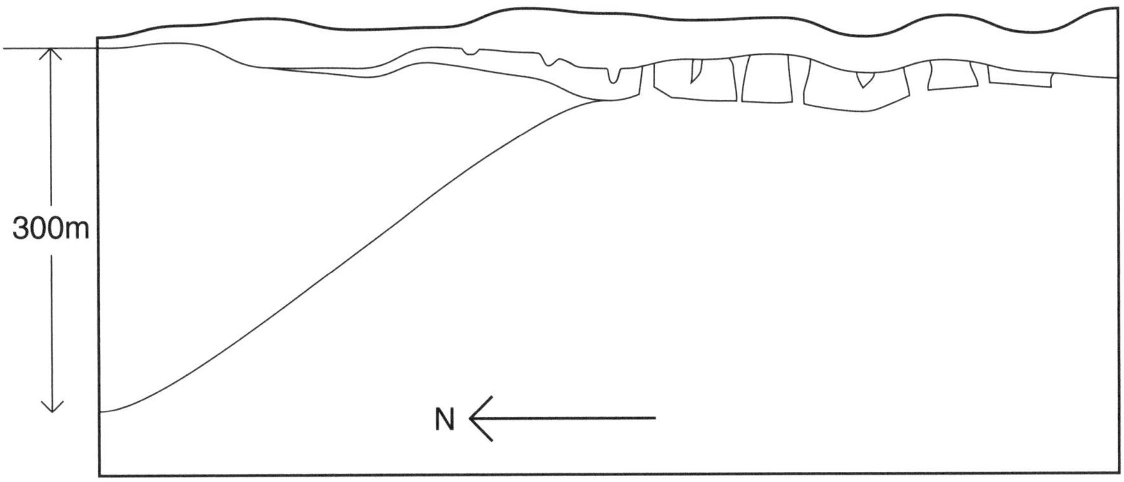


| | | |
|---|---|---|
| | Active layer | a thawed surface layer above permafrost |
| | Continuous permafrost | permanently frozen soil that occurs throughout an area |
| | Discontinuous permafrost | an area with patches of permafrost and patches without permafrost |

Figure 2: Cross-section Showing Permafrost Zones

b) In your own words, explain the difference between continuous and discontinuous permafrost.

______________________________________________

______________________________________________

______________________________________________

______________________________________________

______________________________________________

______________________________________________

c) Explain why the zone of discontinuous permafrost is located to the south of the continuous zone.

_______________________________________________

_______________________________________________

_______________________________________________

_______________________________________________

_______________________________________________

3. a) In the space below, sketch the scene shown in **Figure 5.9** on page 45 of *Geography Now*.

Figure 3: Utilidors in Inuvik, NWT

b) Label the following details in your sketch:
- main neighbourhood utilidors
- household utilidors
- power lines
- houses

4. In what season of the year was the photograph in **Figure 5.9** in *Geography Now* taken? Explain your answer.

_______________________________________________

_______________________________________________

5. Explain why the power lines are not inside the utilidors.

 

## 6.1 Protecting Lands and Natural Systems

**How I Am Being Assessed** ______________________________

______________________________

Read pages 48 to 52 in *Geography Now*. Complete the following sentences as you read.

1. The federal government sits in Ottawa, Ontario, and ______________________________

______________________________

2. The provincial governments meet in their capital cities and ______________________________

______________________________

3. The federal government can protect nature in two ways:

   a) ______________________________

   b) ______________________________

4. National parks are designed to do three things:

   a) ______________________________

   b) ______________________________

   c) ______________________________

   ______________________________

5. Canada's first national park was created in 1883 in Alberta. It was called

______________________________

6. The main idea in a passage may be followed by supporting ideas, which can include

   a) ______________ b) ______________

   c) ______________ d) ______________

7. The Landsat system records images of the earth's surface using

______________________________

# 6.2 Advocating for the Environment

**How I Am Being Assessed** ______________________________

______________________________

*Carefully read these five examples of acting as an advocate for the environment:*

i. You point out to friends that walking to school is better than asking someone to drive you.

ii. You write a letter to the bus company to complain about school buses idling for too long in front of the school.

iii. You encourage some friends to join you in a neighbourhood tree-planting project.

iv. You give a presentation to elementary students about not littering and using refillable drink containers.

v. You join a peaceful demonstration protesting a proposed new roadway that would cross a wetland area near your home.

*Carefully read these five examples that DO NOT illustrate being an advocate for the environment:*

i. You ride your bike to school even though someone would have driven you if you wanted.

ii. Your friends leave their garbage in the cafeteria, and you pick it up for them and put it in the trash container.

iii. You and a friend spend a day cleaning up the garbage along the side of a roadway.

iv. You take over the job of sorting the recyclable materials in your household.

v. You take a hike through a nearby forest to see the wildlife and vegetation.

1. Now write down a definition of what it means to be an advocate for the environment.

______________________________

______________________________

______________________________

______________________________

2. Put a checkmark (✓) next to each sentence below that shows you acting as an advocate for the environment, and an X next to each sentence where you are not acting as an advocate for the environment.

_____ i. You encourage your neighbours not to spray pesticides on their lawns and gardens.

_____ ii. You always buy shampoos and conditioners that are safe for the environment.

_____ iii. You join an environmental group and help them with their campaigns to protect the environment.

_____ iv. You teach your younger brother and his friends to sort their garbage and to recycle everything that they can.

_____ v. You turn off lights when you leave a room and don't let the water run when you are brushing your teeth.

## 6.3 People Power: Greenpeace Action

**How I Am Being Assessed** ______________________________

______________________________________________________

1. Read this article.

### Greenpeace Shuts Down Range Rover Assembly Line

**Production of climate-wrecking SUVs stopped**

*16 May 2005*

*Solihull, United Kingdom*

Early this morning 35 volunteers from Greenpeace shut down the Land Rover assembly line that makes gas-guzzling Range Rovers. The urban 4x4s made at the site are wrecking the climate.

The volunteers used safety shut-down buttons to cut off power to the assembly line before handcuffing and chaining themselves to unfinished vehicles along the 150 m long assembly line. They branded the factory a climate crime scene. It's the first time anywhere in the world that protesters have shut down a factory making sports utility vehicles.

The Range Rover is the UK's least fuel-efficient 4x4, doing a criminal 12 miles to the gallon [23.7 litres per 100 km] in urban areas. The new Range Rover Sport does fewer miles to the gallon than the Model T Ford built 80 years ago.

Making cars like this for urban use is crazy. Most Land Rovers will tackle nothing steeper than a speed bump. Yet Land Rover aggressively markets its range of 4x4s—like Discovery and Range Rover—in towns and cities throughout the UK.

In the UK, road transport accounts for about a quarter of the emissions that cause climate change. The trend of using 4x4 vehicles as urban run-arounds is increasing the amount of emissions going into the atmosphere.

There is no future and no jobs in making cars that wreck the climate. Land Rover has the technology to develop far more fuel-efficient vehicles but they choose not to. It's time for Land Rover to stop making gas-guzzlers.

[Adapted from an article at www.greenpeace.org/international/news/range-rover-shut. No author identified.]

2. Underline or highlight the sentence that contains the main idea in this article.

3. Use the information in the article to answer these questions:

   Who? ______________________________

   What? ______________________________

   When? ______________________________

   Where? ______________________________

   Why? ______________________________

   ______________________________

4. Describe the actions taken by Greenpeace as they were advocating for the environment.

   ______________________________

   ______________________________

   ______________________________

   ______________________________

   ______________________________

5. In your experience, are most SUVs in Canada used mainly for driving on city streets? Should we be concerned about exhaust emissions? Explain your answers.

   ______________________________

   ______________________________

   ______________________________

   ______________________________

6. Do you think that Greenpeace's action were right? Give reasons to support your opinion.

   ______________________________

   ______________________________

   ______________________________

   ______________________________

# PT 1.1 Preparing for Natural Disasters

**How I Am Being Assessed** ______________________________

______________________________

1. List all the different disasters that could affect your region of Canada, using the categories shown in **Figure 1** below.

| Winter | Spring/Summer/Fall | Tectonic |
|---|---|---|
| | | |
| | | |
| | | |
| | | |
| | | |
| | | |

Figure 1: Possible Disasters in My Region of Canada

2. List three major roads or highways in your community.

______________________________

______________________________

______________________________

3. What is the population of your region?

______________________________

4. What major rivers, streams, or lakes surround your community?

______________________________

______________________________

______________________________

5. What is the largest nearby facility that could accommodate a large number of people?

______________________________________________

______________________________________________

______________________________________________

6. How far is it to the nearest

fire station: ________ km

ambulance station: ________ km

hospital: ________ km

7. Who is the mayor or person in charge of your community?

______________________________________________

8. What lifelines do people rely on in your community?

______________________________________________

______________________________________________

______________________________________________

______________________________________________

______________________________________________

______________________________________________

______________________________________________

# Unit 2 HUMAN SYSTEMS

## 7.1 Aboriginal Population Patterns

**How I Am Being Assessed** ______________________________

______________________________________________

1. a) What percentage of the population in each province or territory is Aboriginal? Use the following formula to calculate the percentages:

$$\frac{\text{Aboriginal population}}{\text{Total population}} \times 100$$

For Newfoundland and Labrador, the calculation would look like this:

$$\frac{18\,755}{522\,000} \times 100 = 3.6$$

This answer has been filled in for you in the column headed "Percentage of Aboriginal People in Total Population" in **Figure 1**. Now calculate the percentage for each province or territory and complete the rest of that column.

| Province/Territory | Total Population 2001 | Total Aboriginal Population 2001 | Percentage of Aboriginal People in Total Population | Category |
|---|---|---|---|---|
| Newfoundland and Labrador | 522 000 | 18 775 | 3.6 | |
| Prince Edward Island | 137 000 | 1 345 | | |
| Nova Scotia | 932 000 | 17 010 | | |
| New Brunswick | 750 000 | 16 990 | | |
| Quebec | 7 397 000 | 79 400 | | |
| Ontario | 11 898 000 | 188 315 | | |
| Manitoba | 1 151 000 | 150 045 | | |
| Saskatchewan | 1 000 000 | 130 185 | | |
| Alberta | 3 057 000 | 156 225 | | |
| British Columbia | 4 078 000 | 170 025 | | |
| Yukon Territory | 30 000 | 6 540 | | |
| Northwest Territories | 41 000 | 18 730 | | |
| Nunavut | 29 000 | 22 720 | | |
| **Canada** | 31 021 000 | 976 305 | | |

Figure 1: Aboriginal Population as a Percentage of Total Population of Canada (based on 2001 census data)

b) What patterns do you see in these percentages? We can get a better sense of the patterns by creating categories. Here are the categories to use:

| | | |
|---|---|---|
| ☐ | Very low | Less than 2.0% |
| ☐ | Low | 2.1 to 4.0% |
| ☐ | Medium | 4.1 to 6.0% |
| ☐ | High | Greater than 6.1% |

Choose a colour for each category. Then go back to the table in **Figure 1** and colour in all the boxes in the Category column with the colours you choose.

c) Colour each province and territory in the outline map of Canada (**Figure 2**) in the colour that you assigned to it in the Category column in **Figure 1**.

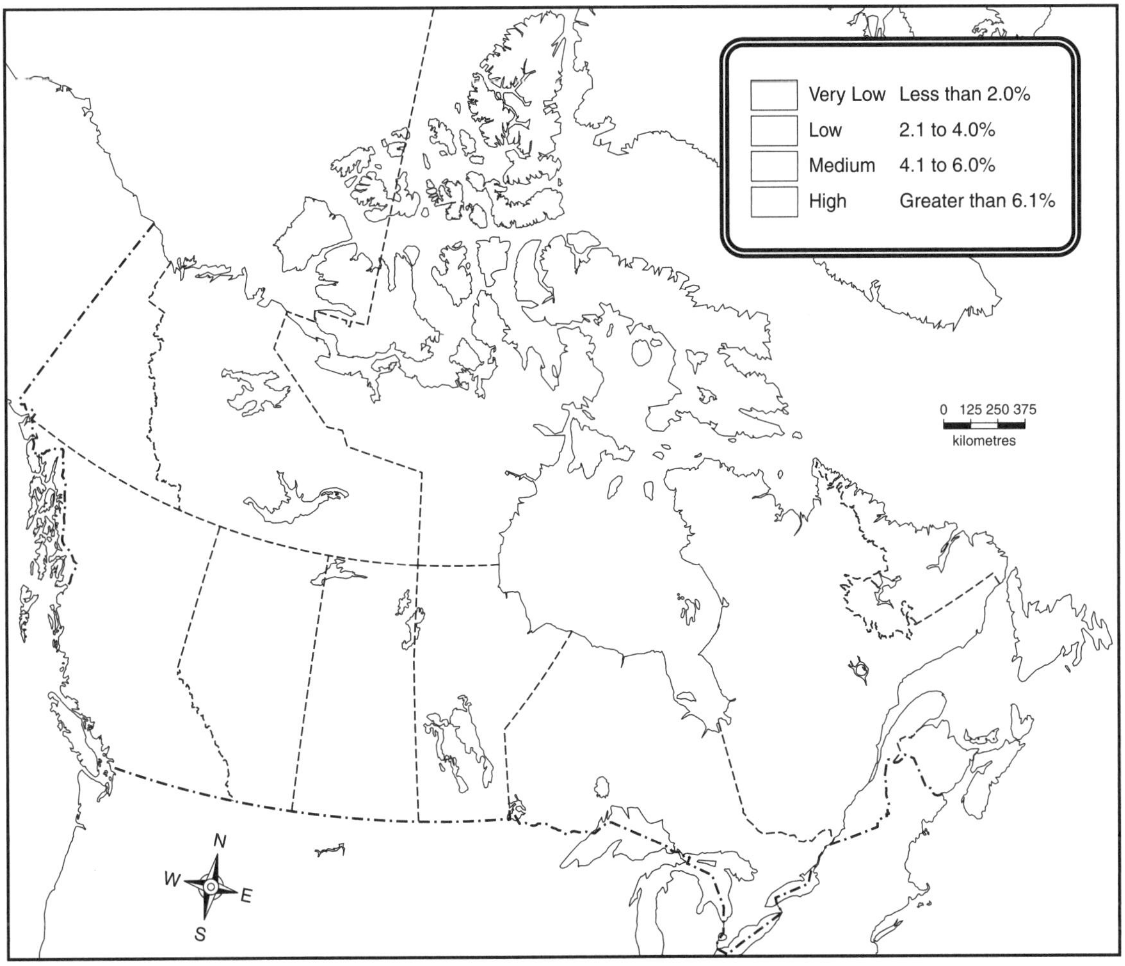


Figure 2: Aboriginal Population by Province and Territory, 2001

d) Which parts of Canada have the highest percentage of Aboriginal peoples?

______________________________________________

## 7.2 Aboriginal Land Claims

**How I Am Being Assessed** ______________________________

______________________________

1. a) Before looking at *Geography Now*, fill in the middle column of the chart in **Figure 1**, writing what you think each of the terms means.

| Term | What I Think It Means | Definition from *Geography Now* |
|---|---|---|
| **treaties** | | |
| **land claims** | | |
| **specific land claims** | | |
| **comprehensive land claims** | | |

Figure 1: Definitions Chart

b) Read pages 65 to 67 of *Geography Now*. Then complete the column on the right, using the Glossary in that book.

c) Which term caused you the most difficulty? Why? ______________________________

______________________________

2. Study the map in **Figure 7.6** on page 65 of *Geography Now*. Identify at least two parts of Canada where Aboriginal peoples did not sign treaties.

______________________________

______________________________

3. a) Read the Case Study below from page 67 of *Geography Now*.

## Treaty Rights to Fish Year Round

In 1993, a man went fishing for eels in Pomquet Harbour, Nova Scotia. The Department of Fisheries and Oceans charged him for fishing without a licence and for fishing when it wasn't eel season. Donald Marshall, Jr., admitted that he had done these things. He fought the charges all the way to the Supreme Court of Canada.

Marshall is a member of the Mi'kmaq First Nation. He argued that, as a member of the Mi'kmaq First Nation, he had a treaty right to fish. A 1760 treaty gave Mi'kmaq and Wolastoqiyik First Nations the right to earn a "moderate living" by fishing and hunting year round. In 1999, Marshall was acquitted by the Supreme Court.

The Supreme Court decision unleashed anger between Aboriginal and non-Aboriginal fishers in the area. The non-Aboriginal fishers felt that all the fish were going to be scooped up by Mi'kmaq fishers. Tensions were so high that the Supreme Court clarified the ruling a few weeks later. It said that the Department of Fisheries and Oceans still had the right to regulate the fishery to conserve the fish. The Aboriginal fishers agreed to honour the government ruling.

b) Circle the words that tell which laws were broken, and label the circles "Laws Broken."

c) Put a box around the words that give Donald Marshall's explanation for his actions and label it "Explanation." (Donald Marshall is the man in the grey shirt in the second row of the picture in **Figure 7.7** on page 66.)

d) Highlight or shade the words that tell what happened after the Supreme Court decision. Label this highlighted part "Consequences."

e) Do you think that Donald Marshall was right when he broke the law? Explain your opinion. ________________________________________

________________________________________________________

________________________________________________________

## 7.3 Developing Transportation in Nunavut

**How I Am Being Assessed** ______________________________

______________________________________________

1. You work for the government of Nunavut and have been asked to decide whether a new port for shipping minerals should be located at Iqaluit, Kugluktuk, or Chesterfield Inlet. The following steps will help you reach a decision. Hint: The maps in **Figures 7.9** to **7.12** on pages 69 and 70 of *Geography Now* will help you locate these communities and identify location factors.

   a) Identify five location factors that you need to consider when making your decision (for example, is the place located close to mineral deposits?). Record these factors in the left-hand column of **Figure 1**.

   b) Score each of the three places on each factor, writing the scores in the chart. Give the best place for that factor a score of 3 and the worst place a score of 1.

   c) Add up the scores for each location. The place with the highest score is the best location for the port.

| | Possible Locations (Scoring: 3 = best; 1 = worst) | | |
|---|---|---|---|
| **Factors To Be Considered** | **Iqaluit** | **Kugluktuk** | **Chesterfield Inlet** |
| 1. | | | |
| 2. | | | |
| 3. | | | |
| 4. | | | |
| 5. | | | |
| **Total Score** | | | |

Figure 1: Decision-making Chart

d) Give two reasons to explain why you chose the place you did.

i. ______________________________

ii. ______________________________

e) Would the same factors be important if you were thinking about building a port to attract cruise ships? Explain your answer.

______________________________

______________________________

2. What are two transportation challenges for Nunavut?

a) ______________________________

______________________________

b) ______________________________

3. **Using the Internet.** Use the Internet to find information on one of these topics:

- challenges for transportation in Nunavut
- opportunities for tourism in Nunavut

Make point-form notes in this space.

______________________________

______________________________

______________________________

______________________________

______________________________

______________________________

______________________________

______________________________

______________________________

# 8.1 Immigration Patterns

**How I Am Being Assessed** ____________________

____________________

1. What does the term *net migration* mean?

____________________

2. a) Using the numbers provided in **Figure 8.4** on page 75 of *Geography Now*, complete **Figure 1** below by

   i. drawing and labelling a line showing total population growth rate

   ii. drawing and labelling a line showing net migration rate

   iii. shading the space between the two lines and labelling it "Natural Increase Rate"

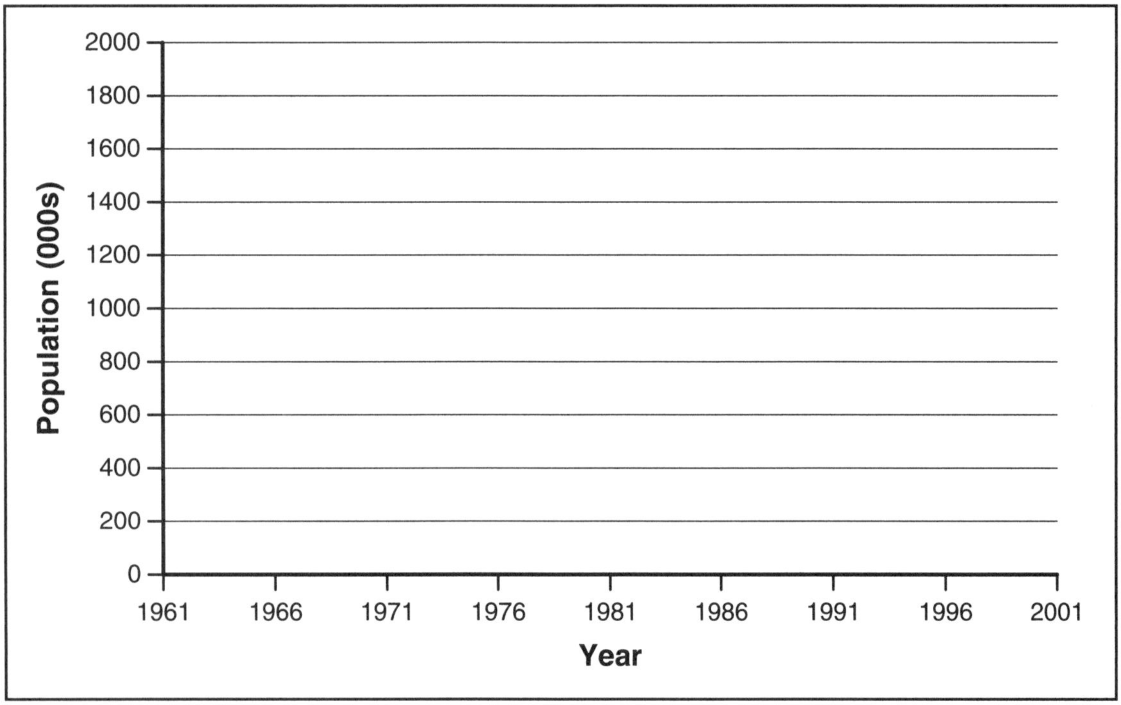


Figure 1: Population Growth, 1961–2001

b) In which period did Canada's population growth increase the most?

____________________

c) In which period was net migration larger than natural increase? ____________

d) In which period was the natural increase the greatest? ____________

## 8.2 Factors That Affect Immigration

**How I Am Being Assessed** ______________________________

______________________________________________________

Fill in the chart below, using the information provided in **Figure 8.7** on page 80. Give the name of each factor and write a brief explanation of how it affects immigration.

**Factors That Affect Immigration**

**Push Factors**

**Pull Factors**

## 8.3 Destinations for Immigrants to Canada

**How I Am Being Assessed** ________________________________

________________________________________________

1. Look at the destination patterns for immigrants in **Figure 8.10** on page 83 of *Geography Now*. Complete the statistical table in **Figure 1** by adding the numbers for some of the regions together.

| Regions | Toronto | Vancouver | Montreal |
|---|---|---|---|
| **Asia** (add East Asia, Southeast Asia and Pacific, South and Central Asia, and Western Asia and the Middle East) | | | |
| **Africa** | | | |
| **Europe** (add Eastern Europe, Western Europe, and the United Kingdom) | | | |
| **Americas** (add Latin America, the Caribbean, and the United States) | | | |

Figure 1: Origins of Recent Immigrants to Large Cities, 2001, as Percentage of Immigrants. Totals may not equal 100% due to rounding.

2. In **Figure 2**, draw a divided bar graph to show the data in **Figure 1**. Shade each region a different colour. (A divided bar graph stacks each region on top of the previous ones, for a total of 100 percent. The regions must be in the same order in each bar. For an example of this type of graph, see **Figure 14.7** in *Geography Now*.) The divisions for Toronto have been marked for you.

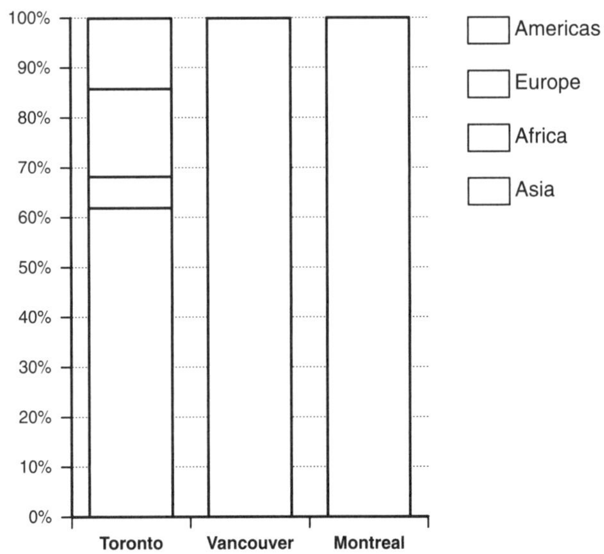


Figure 2: Origins of Recent Immigrants, 2001

3. a) Explain why a divided (or stacked) bar graph is a good way to compare percentages.

b) Why do you suppose Africa is the smallest source region for each of the three places?

c) Why do you suppose Asia is the largest source region for each of the three places?

d) Why do you suppose the percentage of Asian immigrants going to Montreal is so much less than the percentage going to Vancouver?

4. On page 76 of *Geography Now* we see that immigration from Asia has been growing. Predict how the divided bar graphs for these cities might be different in 2021.

# 9.1 Population Distribution

**How I Am Being Assessed** ______________________________

______________________________

1. Write a definition for *population distribution.*

______________________________

______________________________

Figure 1: The Distribution of Canada's Population, 1871. The lines on the map were the provincial boundaries at the time.

2. Put an X on the map in **Figure 1** above to show where you live in Canada.

3. Use distribution words from **Figure 9.3** on page 88 of *Geography Now* to describe Canada's population distribution in 1871.

______________________________

______________________________

______________________________

4. Compare the map in **Figure 9.2** on page 87 of *Geography Now* with the map of population distribution in 1871 in **Figure 1** on the previous page of your workbook. In **Figure 2** below, record two patterns that have changed and two that have remained the same.

| Two Patterns That Have Stayed the Same | Two Patterns That Have Changed |
|---|---|
| | |
| | |

Figure 2: Comparison of Regional Populations

5. In the spaces in **Figure 3** below, write short notes to explain how each of the factors might affect population distribution.

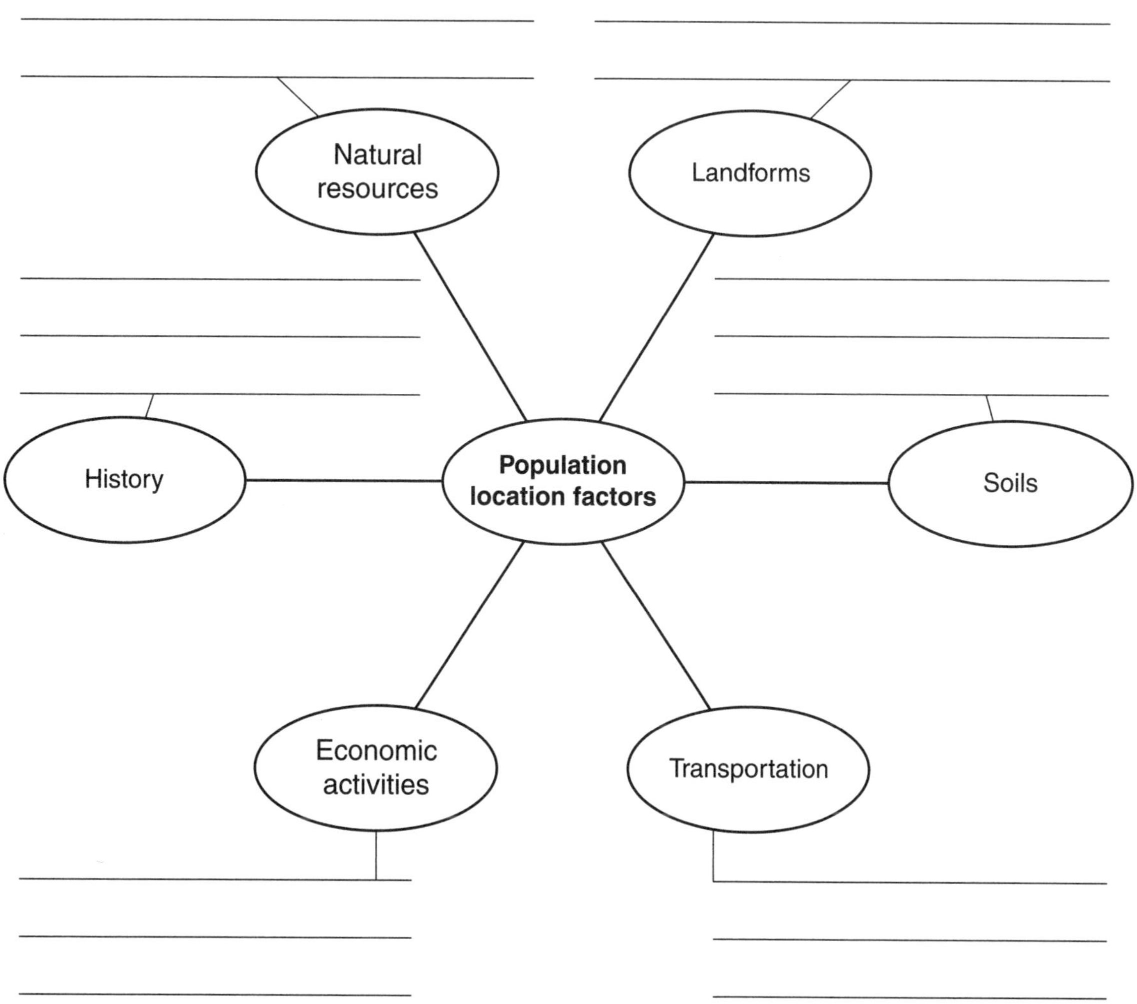


Figure 3: Factors That Affect Population Distribution

6. a) Use the information in **Figure 9.5** on page 88 of *Geography Now* to calculate the percentage change in the populations of provinces and territories between 1991 and 2005. Calculate the percentage change for each province and territory in this way:

$$\frac{\text{(Change 1991–2005)}}{\text{(Population 1991)}} \times 100$$

Ontario's percentage change would be calculated using these numbers:

$$\frac{2\,113}{10\,428} \times 100 = 20.3\%$$

Record your percentage change figures in the right-hand column of **Figure 4** below.

| **Province/Territory** | **1991 (000s)** | **2005 (000s)** | **Change 1991–2005 (000s)** | **Percent Population Change 1991–2005** |
|---|---|---|---|---|
| **Newfoundland and Labrador** | 580 | 516 | −64 | |
| **Prince Edward Island** | 130 | 138 | 8 | |
| **Nova Scotia** | 915 | 938 | 23 | |
| **New Brunswick** | 746 | 752 | 6 | |
| **Quebec** | 7 065 | 7 598 | 533 | |
| **Ontario** | 10 428 | 12 541 | 2 113 | 20.3 |
| **Manitoba** | 1 110 | 1 178 | 68 | |
| **Saskatchewan** | 1 003 | 994 | −9 | |
| **Alberta** | 2 593 | 3 257 | 664 | |
| **British Columbia** | 3 373 | 4 254 | 881 | |
| **Yukon Territory** | 29 | 31 | 2 | |
| **Northwest Territories** | 39 | 43 | 4 | |
| **Nunavut** | 22 | 30 | 8 | |

Figure 4: Percentage Population Change, 1991–2005

b) Point out two patterns you can observe in the percentage population changes of the provinces and territories.

i. ______________________________

______________________________

______________________________

ii. ______________________________________________

______________________________________________

c) Draw a divergent bar graph in **Figure 5** below, using the percentage change numbers that you calculated for **Figure 4**. Where a province's population has decreased, the number is negative and the bar you draw should go toward the left of the zero axis (see the bar already drawn for Saskatchewan). Where a province's population has grown, the number is positive and the bar you draw should go toward the right of the zero axis (see the bar already drawn for Ontario). (For an example of this type of graph, see **Figure 20.8** in *Geography Now*.)

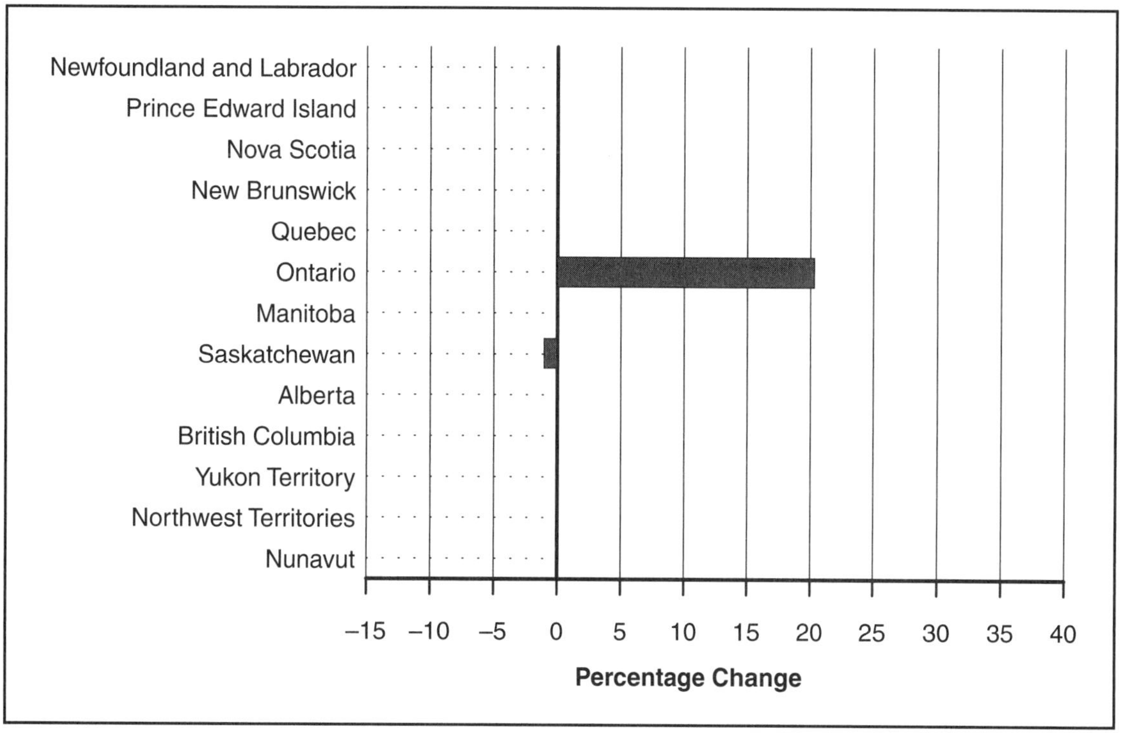


Figure 5: ______________________________________________

d) Supply a title for your graph.

e) How does presenting information in a graph of this type allow you to interpret trends more easily?

______________________________________________

______________________________________________

## 9.2 Population Density

**How I Am Being Assessed** ______________________________

______________________________________________________

1. Population density is the average number of people in each square kilometre of a place. For each of the four squares in **Figure 1**, write in the population density that is shown.

Population Density = ________ people/km$^2$

Population Density = ________ people/km$^2$

Population Density = ________ people/km$^2$

Population Density = ________ people/km$^2$

Figure 1: The Concept *Population Density*

2. a) Calculate the population densities for each province and territory using the data in **Figure 2**. Put the density numbers in the third column, labelled Population Density.

Density is calculated in this way:

$$\text{Population Density} = \frac{\text{Population}}{\text{Area}}$$

The population density of Newfoundland and Labrador would be calculated like this:

$$\frac{\text{Population}}{\text{Area}} = \frac{516\ 000}{405\ 212} = 1.3$$

This answer has been filled in for you in the column headed Population Density in **Figure 2**. Now calculate the population density of each province or territory and complete the rest of that column.

| Province/Territory | Population | Area of Province | Population Density | Colour |
|---|---|---|---|---|
| Newfoundland and Labrador | 516 000 | 405 212 | 1.3 | |
| Prince Edward Island | 138 000 | 5 660 | | |
| Nova Scotia | 938 000 | 55 284 | | |
| New Brunswick | 752 000 | 72 908 | | |
| Quebec | 7 598 000 | 1 542 056 | | |
| Ontario | 12 541 000 | 1 076 395 | | |
| Manitoba | 1 178 000 | 647 797 | | |
| Saskatchewan | 994 000 | 651 036 | | |
| Alberta | 3 257 000 | 661 848 | | |
| British Columbia | 4 254 000 | 944 735 | | |
| Yukon Territory | 31 000 | 482 443 | | |
| Northwest Territories | 43 000 | 1 346 106 | | |
| Nunavut | 30 000 | 2 093 190 | | |

Figure 2: Population Density, 2005

b) Which province or territory has the highest population density?

_______________________________________________

c) Which region of Canada has the lowest density? ____________________

d) Use four coloured pencils to colour the map in **Figure 3** to match your population density calculations. Follow the following procedure:

i. Shade each box in the legend on the map a different colour.

ii. Identify which box in the legend fits the population density of a particular province or territory.

iii. Colour the appropriate block in the fourth column in **Figure 2** in the same colour you used in the legend.

iv. Repeat for all the provinces and territories.

v. Using the colours in column 4 as a guide, colour in each province and territory on the map in **Figure 3**.

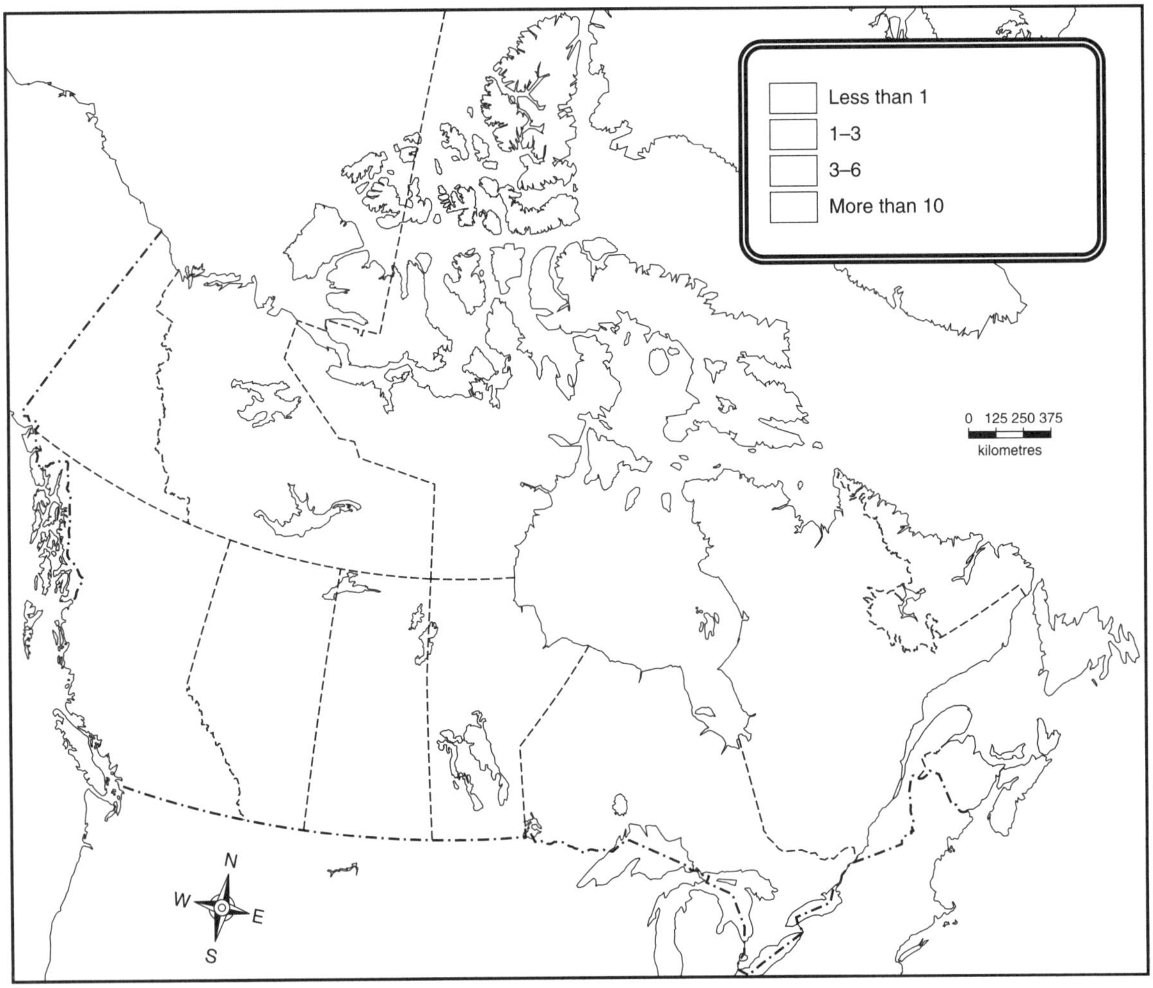


Figure 3: Population Densities in Canada

3. Write a definition for *population density*.

______________________________________________

______________________________________________

# 9.3 Rural-to-Urban Migration

**How I Am Being Assessed** ______________________________

______________________________________________________

1. Draw and label two sketches. The first sketch should show the characteristics of a rural area. The second sketch should show the characteristics of an urban area.

**Rural Area**

**Urban Area**

Figure 1: Characteristics of an Urban Area and a Rural Area

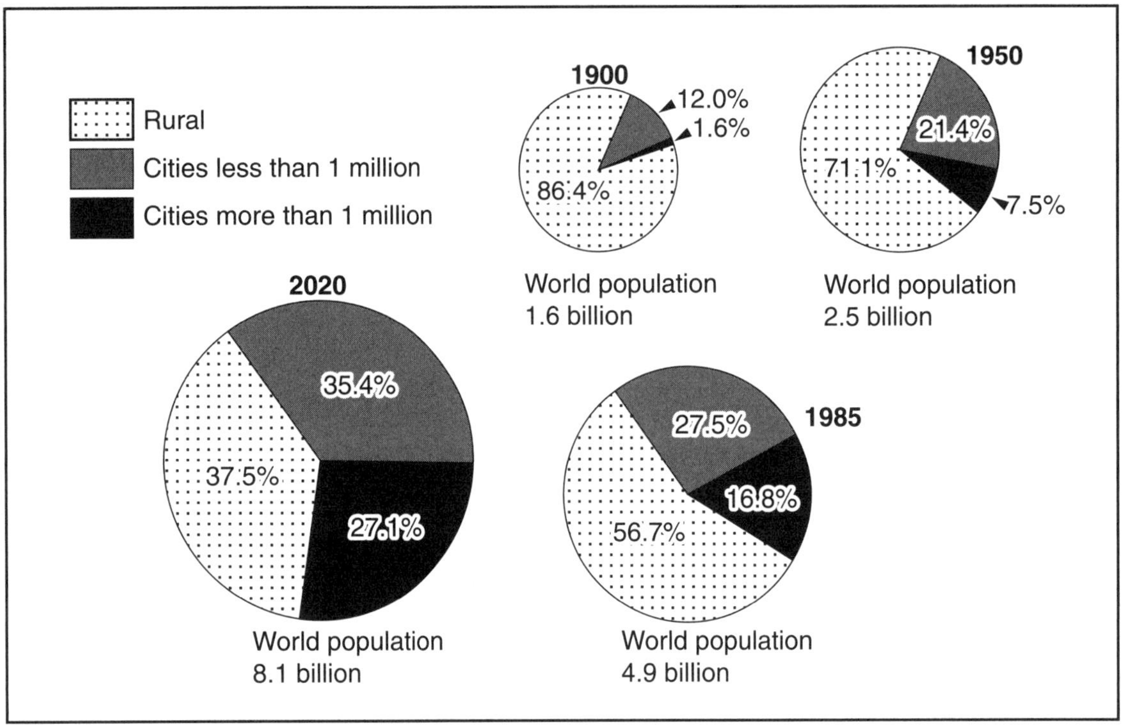


Figure 2: Global Patterns of Rural-to-Urban Migration

2. a) What do the different sizes of the circles show in **Figure 2** above?

______________________________________________

b) What are two patterns that the circle graphs show about global rural-to-urban migration?

i. ______________________________________________

______________________________________________

ii. ______________________________________________

______________________________________________

3. In what ways is Canada's situation the same as and different from the global pattern of rural-to-urban migration? (Hint: Look at **Figure 9.6** in *Geography Now*.)

______________________________________________

______________________________________________

______________________________________________

4. Predict two possible consequences for the natural environment of the growth of large cities.

a) ______________________________________________

______________________________________________

______________________________________________

b) ______________________________________________

______________________________________________

______________________________________________

5. **Using the Internet**. What is *urban sprawl*? Why do some people think that urban sprawl is a problem?

______________________________________________

______________________________________________

______________________________________________

______________________________________________

______________________________________________

______________________________________________

______________________________________________

______________________________________________

______________________________________________

______________________________________________

______________________________________________

______________________________________________

## 9.4 An Aging Population

**How I Am Being Assessed** ____________________

____________________

1. a) Use the statistical information in **Figure 9.13** on page 95 of *Geography Now* to construct a divided bar graph for the years 1951, 1981, 2001, and 2016. Shade each age group a different colour. The divisions on the bar for 1951 have been marked for you. (For an example of this type of graph, see **Figure 14.7** in *Geography Now*.)

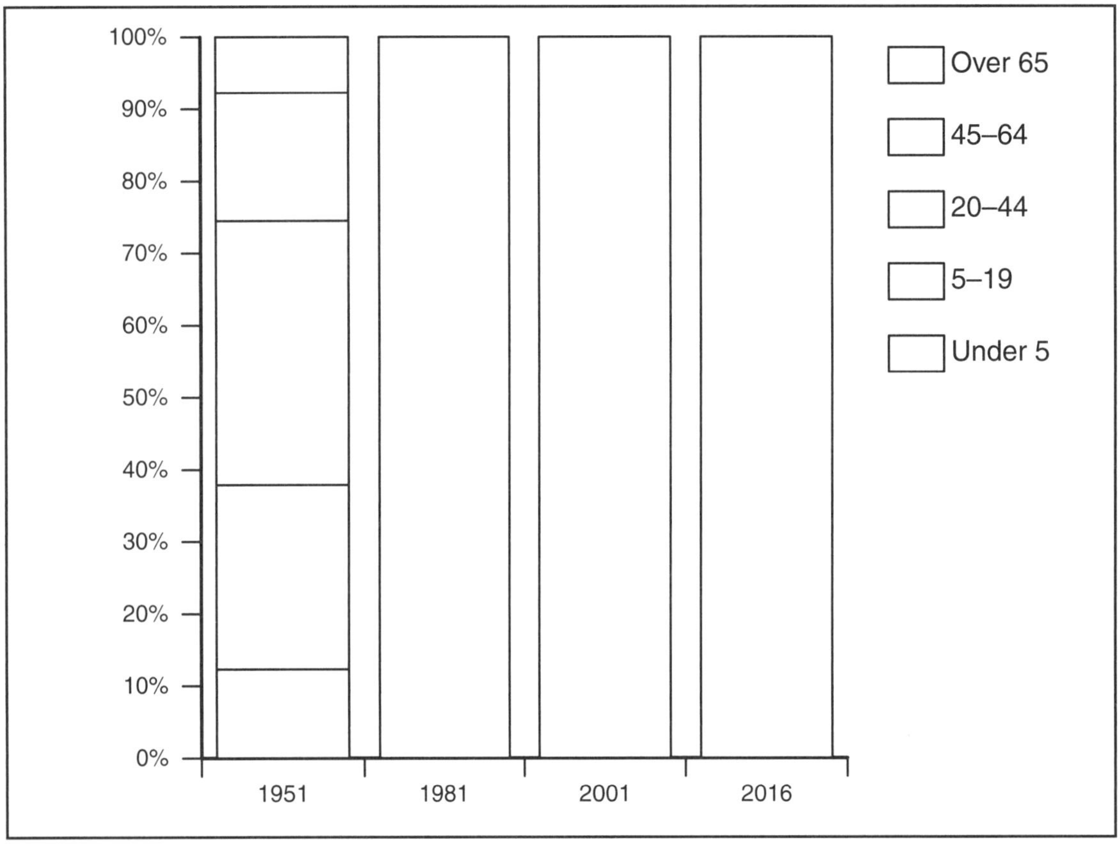


Figure 1: Age Structure of Canada's Population, 1951–2016

b) Make two observations about patterns in your divided bar graph.

i. ____________________

____________________

ii. ____________________

c) How do you explain the steady downward trend in the percentage of Canadians under 5 years old?

______________________________________________________________

______________________________________________________________

2. a) Use the information in **Figure 2** below to construct a population pyramid similar to the one in **Figure 9.14** on page 95 of *Geography Now*.

| Age Group | % Males | % Females | Age Group | % Males | % Females |
|---|---|---|---|---|---|
| 0–4 | 2.7 | 2.6 | 50–54 | 3.5 | 3.5 |
| 5–9 | 3.1 | 2.9 | 55–59 | 3.0 | 3.0 |
| 10–14 | 3.4 | 3.2 | 60–64 | 2.2 | 2.3 |
| 15–19 | 3.4 | 3.2 | 65–69 | 1.8 | 1.9 |
| 20–24 | 3.6 | 3.4 | 70–74 | 1.5 | 1.7 |
| 25–29 | 3.4 | 3.3 | 75–79 | 1.1 | 1.5 |
| 30–34 | 3.5 | 3.4 | 80–84 | 0.7 | 1.2 |
| 35–39 | 3.8 | 3.7 | 85–89 | 0.3 | 0.6 |
| 40–44 | 4.3 | 4.3 | 90 and over | 0.1 | 0.4 |
| 45-49 | 4.0 | 4.0 | | | |

Figure 2: Canada's Age and Gender Statistics, 2004

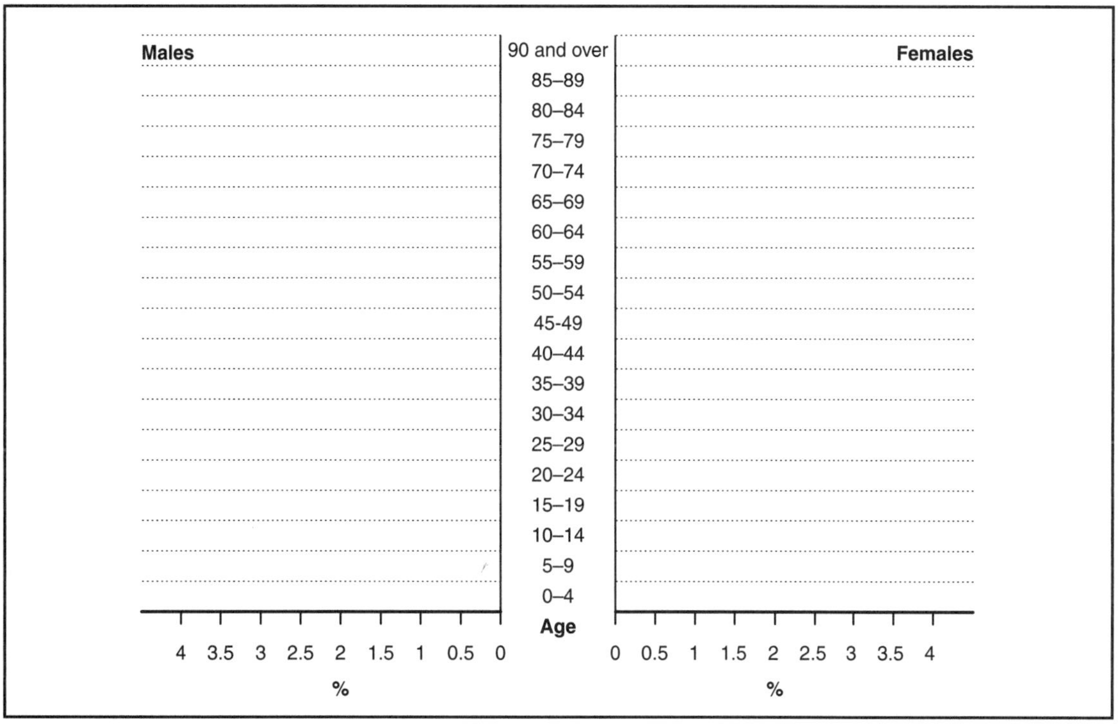


Figure 3: Canada's Population Pyramid, 2004

b) Around what ages were the baby boomers in 2004?

______________________________________________

c) Around what percentage was the bar that represented you in 2004?

______________________________________________

d) Is Canada's birth rate increasing or decreasing, based on the information in your population pyramid? (Look at the bars at the bottom of the graph.)

______________________________________________

e) Predict what the shape of Canada's population pyramid will be 20 years from now. Explain your answer.

______________________________________________

______________________________________________

______________________________________________

______________________________________________

______________________________________________

# 10.1 Changing Urban Patterns

**How I Am Being Assessed** ______________________________

______________________________

You will complete this activity using **Figure 10.4** on page 100 of *Geography Now*.

## Set a Purpose for Reading the Table

1. Write down two general questions about the table.

______________________________

______________________________

## Preview the Table

2. What is the title of the table?

______________________________

3. What are the headings of the columns in this table?

______________________________

4. What units are used in the table?

______________________________

5. Write down and define one new or important term from the table.

______________________________

## Read the Table

6. In general, what is the statistical table telling you?

______________________________

______________________________

______________________________

7. What are three factual statements that you can make on the basis of the information in this table? (For example, you could say that Toronto has the largest population of any CMA in Canada.)

______________________________________________

______________________________________________

______________________________________________

______________________________________________

## After Reading the Table

8. Draw three conclusions or mention three things you can observe from the table. One answer has been filled in for you.

| Conclusion/Observation | Supporting Information |
|---|---|
| Some cities are more spread out than others. | Sherbrooke, QC, and Sudbury have very similar populations, but Sudbury occupies an area three times larger than Sherbrooke. |

9. Make connections by asking, "What does this information mean to me?"

| Information | My Thoughts |
|---|---|
| | |

## Remember

10. Write three short sentences to help you remember things that you learned about interpreting a table or about population growth as you completed this worksheet.

    a) ______________________________

    ______________________________

    ______________________________

    b) ______________________________

    ______________________________

    ______________________________

    c) ______________________________

    ______________________________

    ______________________________

## 10.2 Urban Land Use

**How I Am Being Assessed** ____________________________________

____________________________________________________________

1. As you read pages 101 to 105 of *Geography Now*, try to find a definition and one example of each of the following terms on urban land use.

| Term | Definition | Example |
|---|---|---|
| urban functions | | |
| basic activities | | |
| non-basic activities | | |
| land use | | |
| residential land use | | |
| commercial land use | | |
| urban planners | | |

Figure 1: Important Terms and Definitions

2. Here is a copy of the photograph in **Figure 10.10** on page 104 of *Geography Now*. Look carefully at the coloured photograph there and then label Toronto Harbour on **Figure 2**. Also label examples of the following uses of land:

- transportation
- residential
- commercial
- recreational
- communication

Figure 2: Toronto's Harbour Area

# 10.3 Urban Geography Crossword Puzzle

**How I Am Being Assessed** ______________________________

______________________________________________

Complete this crossword puzzle using words from Chapter 10.

ACROSS

6. This is largely an urban problem
8. The area closest to the camera in a picture
10. Land use category for where people live
12. A CMA located in Manitoba
13. Examples are water lines and power grids
14. People who help design cities
15. Type of change that has affected cities

DOWN

1. Smaller than a village
2. Economic activities in cities are called "urban _______"
3. The most populated CMA in Canada
4. A cause of poverty
5. Another word for "city"
7. Past land use in Toronto's harbour area
9. What the "C" stands for in CBD
11. Town-forming activities

# 11.1 Organizing Ideas About Making Things

**How I Am Being Assessed** ______________________________

______________________________

Read pages 108 to 111 of *Geography Now*. Write down what you consider to be the main idea of this part of the chapter and make point-form notes about the different categories of industries.

**Main Idea**

______________________________

______________________________

______________________________

**Details About Primary Industries**

______________________________

______________________________

______________________________

**Details About Secondary Industries**

______________________________

______________________________

______________________________

**Details About Tertiary Industries**

______________________________

______________________________

______________________________

## 11.2 Understanding Location Factors for Manufacturing

**How I Am Being Assessed** ______________________________

______________________________________________

Read about location factors for manufacturing on pages 112 to 113 of *Geography Now*. Make point-form notes about the location factors in this chart.

**Location Factors for Manufacturing**

| History | Location of markets | Access to raw materials |
|---|---|---|
| | | |

| Labour supply | Transportation |
|---|---|
| | |

 

# 12.1 Chapter Outline

**How I Am Being Assessed** ______________________________

______________________________

An outline helps you to understand the organization of what you are reading. Skim and scan Chapter 12 in *Geography Now* to find words and phrases that identify the main topics and the subtopics. (For information on skimming and scanning, see the Literacy Skill box on page 178 of *Geography Now*.)

**Main Topic**

(Hint: Look for the terms that are emphasized with italics, bullets, or definitions in the Introduction to the chapter.)

______________________________

a) ______________________________

b) ______________________________

c) ______________________________

**Subtopic 1**

(Hint: Look for the first bold subheading in the chapter, and then at any subheadings and definitions between it and the next bold heading.)

______________________________

a) ______________________________

b) ______________________________

c) ______________________________

**Subtopic 2**

______________________________

a) ______________________________

b) ______________________________

c) ______________________________

**Subtopic 3**

______________________________

a) ______________________________

b) ______________________________

c) ______________________________

# 12.2 Mechanization of Agriculture: A Cause–Effect Organizer

**How I Am Being Assessed** ________________________________________

________________________________________________________________

A cause–effect organizer helps you to sort out what are causes and what are effects. Complete this chart using **Figure 12.4** on page 122 of *Geography Now*.

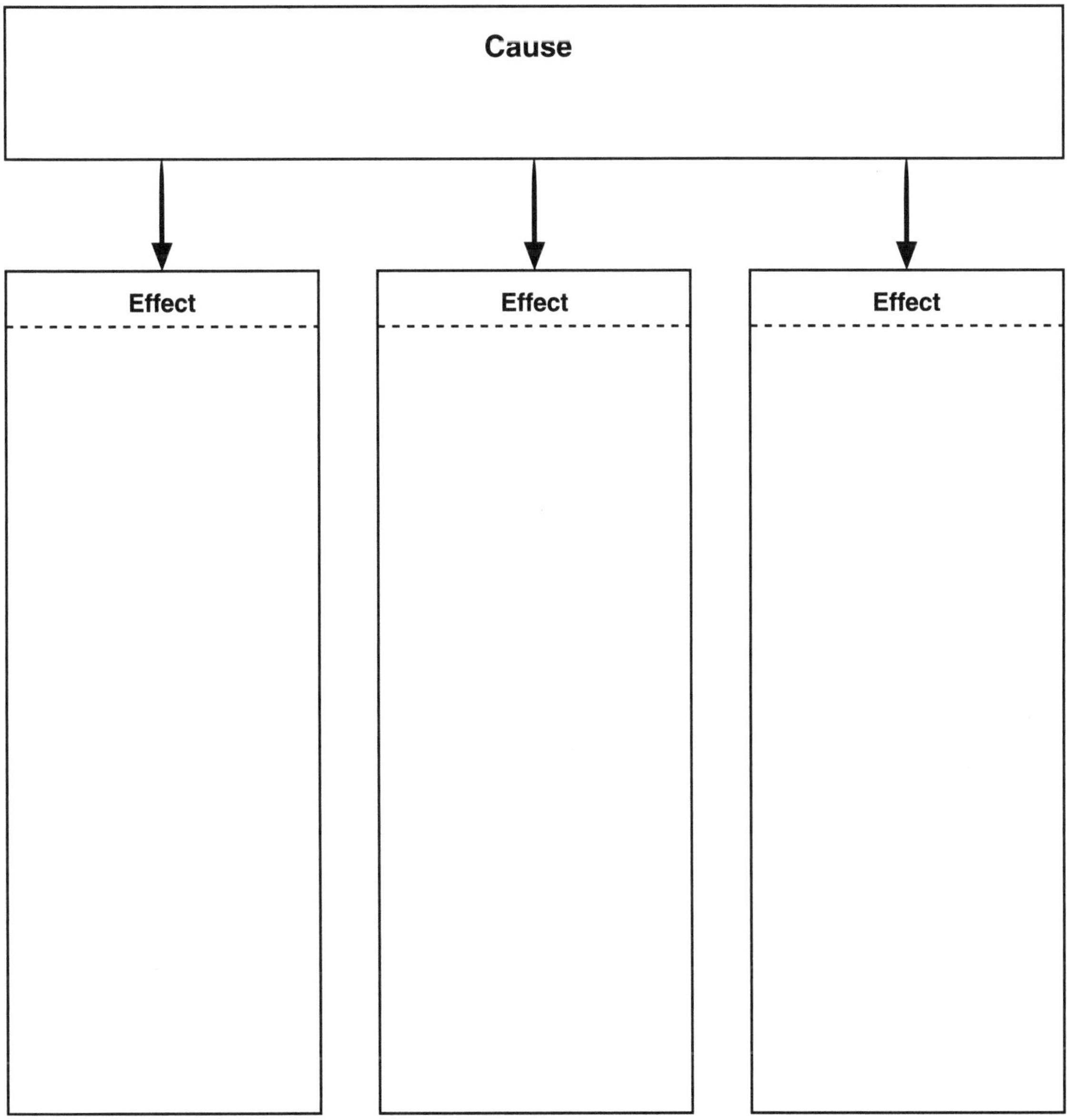


Figure 1: Cause–Effect Organizer

# 12.3 Mapping the Value of Minerals

**How I Am Being Assessed** ______________________________

______________________________________________________

1. Use the statistical table in **Figure 12.8** on page 126 of *Geography Now* to create a map/graph showing the value of the minerals mined in each province and territory in 2003. See **Figure 13.12** on page 139 for an example of a map/graph.
2. Supply a title for your map/graph.

1 cm = $500 million

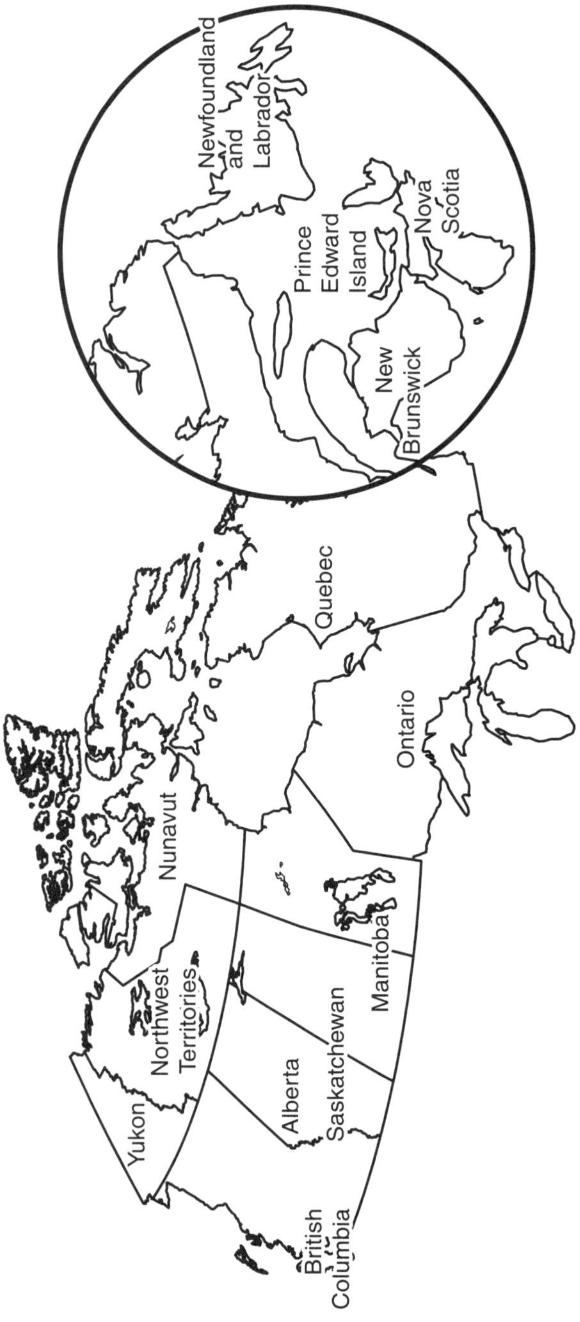


Figure 1: ______________________________

# 13.1 Locating Transportation Services

**How I Am Being Assessed** ______________________________

______________________________

You are part of a team of planners deciding where to locate a new airport in Canada. This airport will be used by people and goods going to and coming from other countries. It will handle huge volumes of cargo and people.

1. a) Three cities have been selected as possible sites. They are Saint John, New Brunswick; Hamilton, Ontario; and Calgary, Alberta. Write the names of these cities in the decision-making organizer in **Figure 1** on the next page.

   b) Fill in four priorities that you must consider. These are the location needs of the airport.

   c) Find information about each of the cities using *Geography Now*, classroom and school resources, and the Internet. Note good and bad points about each location.

   d) Make a decision.

2. a) What city did you decide was the best location?

   ______________________________

   b) Explain why you chose this location.

   ______________________________

   ______________________________

3. Explain why an airport is a tertiary industry.

   ______________________________

4. Why is using a decision-making organizer a good method for making a decision?

   ______________________________

   ______________________________

   ______________________________

**Issue**

Where is the best location for a large international airport?

| Possible locations | Priorities | | | | Consequence (summary) | |
|---|---|---|---|---|---|---|
| | | | | | | |
| | | | | | + | |
| | | | | | – | |
| | | | | | + | |
| | | | | | – | |
| | | | | | + | |
| | | | | | – | |

**Decision**

Figure 1: Decision-making Organizer

# 13.2 Using Your New Vocabulary

**How I Am Being Assessed** ______________________________

______________________________________________________

**Part A: Circle the correct or best answer from the options given.**

1. What is the name given to services that involve making important decisions?

   a) discretionary income

   b) retail sales

   c) quaternary industries

   d) business services

2. Which of these people is working in retail sales?

   a) a cashier in a fast-food restaurant

   b) a bus driver

   c) a teacher

   d) an office cleaner

3. Which of these statements about retail sales is true?

   a) most men in retail sales work part-time

   b) more women than men work in retail sales

   c) more women than men work full-time

   d) about 600 000 women work in retail sales

4. Which is the best way to move bulky goods a long distance over land?

   a) by ship

   b) by truck

   c) by plane

   d) by train

5. Which of these expenses would be part of your discretionary spending? (Discretionary spending is spending on something that you want, but do not need.)

   a) paying to ride the bus to school

   b) going to see a movie with some friends

   c) shopping for groceries for your lunch

   d) buying a winter coat

**Part B: Fill in the missing word in each statement. The answer is on the page given in parentheses.**

6. One of the challenges of working in retail sales is that wages are________. (p. 133)

7. Some stores want to be located near their competitors because customers want to ____________________ products when they shop. (p. 134)

8. Air transport is not always the best method of moving goods because it is expensive and can't handle ____________________________ cargo. (p. 135)

9. The growth of the Internet means that many people can do their jobs by _________________________. (p. 137)

10. The fastest-growing sector of tertiary industries is_________________________ ____________________. (four words, p. 138)

**Part C: Circle T if the statement is true and F if the statement is false.**

| | | |
|---|---|---|
| 11. Quaternary means fourth. | T | F |
| 12. One of the advantages of working in retail sales is that workers get good benefits, such as medical plans. | T | F |
| 13. Infrastructure refers to the basic services that support all economic activities. | T | F |
| 14. About 13 percent of households in Canada do not have telephones. | T | F |
| 15. Most of the services we buy are not essential to life; we buy them because we want them. | T | F |

## 14.1 Regional Disparities

**How I Am Being Assessed** ______________________________

______________________________

1. Fill in the left-hand and middle columns of this K-W-L chart, stating what you know and what you want to know about regional disparities.

| What I Know | What I Want to Know | What I Learned |
|---|---|---|
| | | |
| | | |
| | | |
| | | |
| | | |
| | | |
| | | |
| | | |
| | | |
| | | |
| | | |
| | | |
| | | |
| | | |
| | | |

Figure 1: K-W-L Chart

2. Read pages 142 to 147 of *Geography Now*. Then fill in the right-hand column of the K-W-L chart.

# 14.2 Reasons for Regional Disparities

**How I Am Being Assessed** ______________________________

______________________________

The main idea organizer in **Figure 1** will help you sort out the big ideas and the smaller details. Use the information in **Figure 14.5** on page 144 of *Geography Now* to complete this organizer.

| **Main Idea** | | |
|---|---|---|
| Regional disparities occur because resources are not distributed equally across Canada. | | |
| **Detail**<br>Location | **Detail**<br>Available Resources | **Detail**<br>Government Actions |
| | | |
| **Conclusion** | | |

Figure 1: Main Ideas Organizer

## 14.3 The Health Care Crisis

**How I Am Being Assessed** ______________________________

______________________________________________________

One method of recording details about a source is to make paragraph-by-paragraph notes. You record one important fact from each paragraph or from each illustration in the source.

Read pages 148 to 149 of *Geography Now* and make notes about each paragraph and figure there.

| Paragraph or Figure Number | Facts I Found |
|---|---|
| 1 | |
| 2 | |
| 3 | |
| 4 | |
| 5 | |
| 6 | |
| 7 | |

# PT 2.1 Introduction to Ecozones

**How I Am Being Assessed** ______________________________

______________________________________________

1. What is the definition of an *ecozone*?

______________________________________________

______________________________________________

2. The terms used to refer to landforms come from different sources:

| | |
|---|---|
| **Terms based on landform features** | Cordillera, Plain, Shield |
| **Terms based on climate characteristics** | Arctic, Maritime |
| **Terms based on vegetation** | Mixed-wood, Montane, Prairie, Taiga, Boreal |
| **Terms based on geographic location** | Northern, Southern, Atlantic, Pacific, Hudson Bay |

Figure 1: Terms Used in Ecozone Names

a) Write down the names of the two ecozones that you are going to research.

i. ______________________________________________

ii. ______________________________________________

b) Identify the sources of the words in the names of your ecozones.

______________________________________________

______________________________________________

______________________________________________

3. **Figure 2** identifies some of the characteristics that are considered in defining ecozones. Write one example or comment next to each characteristic. (For example, for landforms, you might write "plains.")

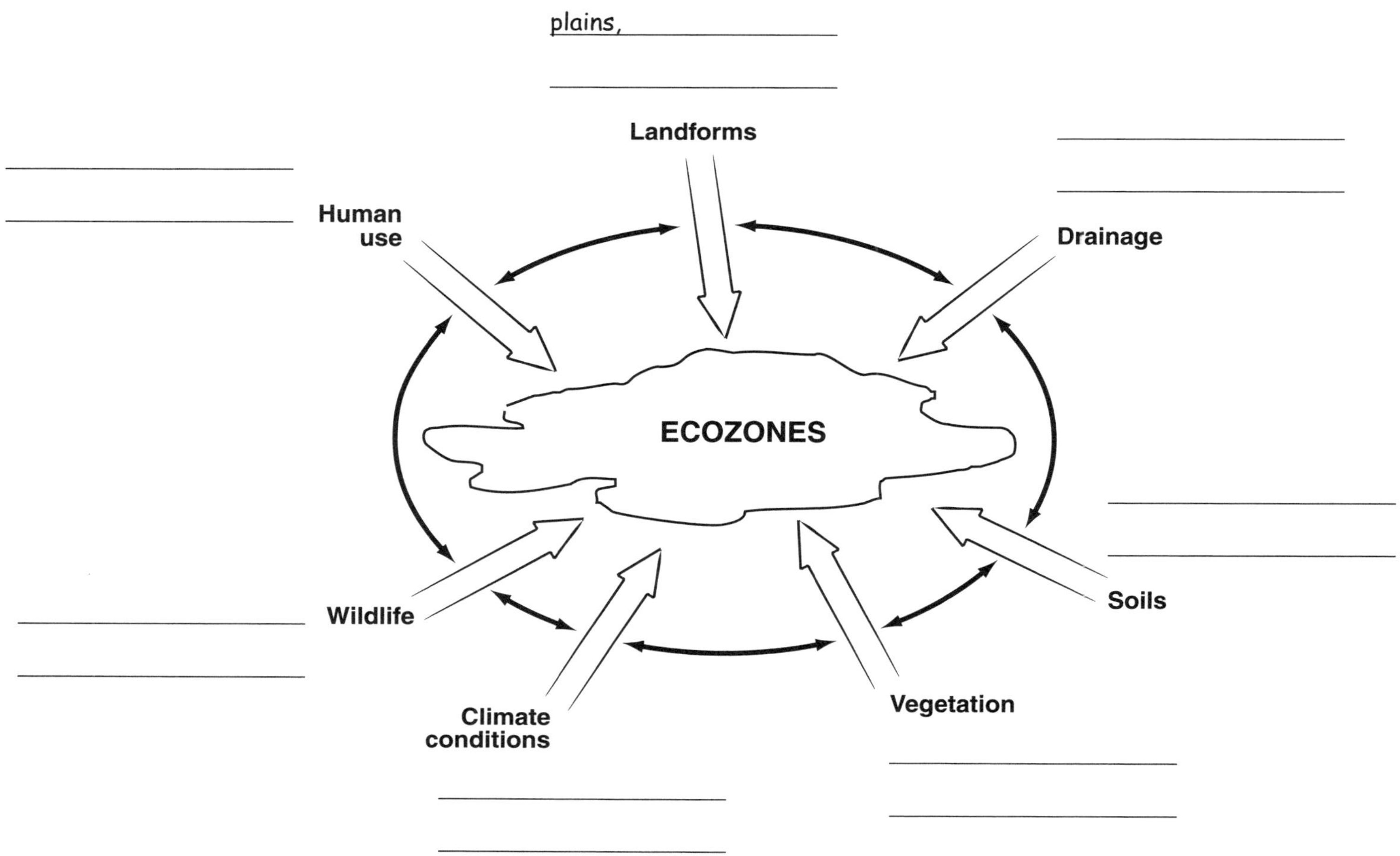


Figure 2: Factors That Affect Ecozones

# Unit 3 ENVIRONMENTAL CHALLENGES

# 15.1 Aboriginal Peoples and the Environment: Introduction

**How I Am Being Assessed** ________________________________________

____________________________________________________________

1. The following scrambled words can all be found in either Chapter 7 or Chapter 15 of *Geography Now*. Unscramble each of the words and write it in the space provided.

| | |
|---|---|
| M L Y F A I | ▢ _ _ _ _ _ |
| I L B G R N O A I A | _ _ _ _ ▢ _ _ _ _ _ |
| R D E L S E | _ _ _ _ ▢ _ |
| O R T I S E S | _ _ _ _ _ _ ▢ |
| E M T T O O L P E | ▢ _ _ _ _ _ _ _ _ |
| D A L N M L I A C | _ _ ▢ _ _ _ _ _ _ |
| I S T T E E R A | _ _ _ ▢ _ _ _ _ |
| T U I I N | _ _ _ _ ▢ |
| G R I T S H | _ ▢ _ _ _ _ |
| T N R O H | _ ▢ _ _ _ |
| U K I N S K U | _ ▢ _ _ _ _ _ |
| L R O A O S I E T H I S Y R | _ _ _ _ _ _ _ _ _ _ _ _ ▢ |

2. Use the letters that are highlighted in the words above to find another word that also relates to the content of this chapter.

_ _ _ _ _    _ _ _ _ _ _ _

## 15.2 Inuksuit and Totem Poles

**How I Am Being Assessed** ______________________________

______________________________

1. Define the term *inuksuk* (plural, *inuksuit*).

______________________________

2. Where in Canada do we find most of the original inuksuit?

______________________________

3. Inuksuit have different functions. In each of the spaces below, draw what you think an inuksuk would look like if it were built for the purpose suggested in the space.

| | |
|---|---|
| | |
| Inuksuk showing direction | Inuksuk showing shelter |
| | |
| Inuksuk showing food storage | Inuksuk showing ___________ (your choice) |

Figure 1: Functions of Inuksuit

4. a) In what province of Canada are most totem poles found?

   b) Why are they found in this province?

5. List some of the common animals or birds that are often shown on totem poles.

6. Using either your own drawings or images from a magazine or the Internet, design a totem pole to represent yourself. It should include at least four different images. In the lines next to **Figure 2**, explain why you have chosen each image. (See the table on page 157 for some ideas.)

a)

b)

c)

d)

Figure 2: My Totem Pole

# 15.3 Traditional Ecological Knowledge

**How I Am Being Assessed** ______________________________

______________________________

1. Define *traditional ecological knowledge* (TEK).

______________________________

______________________________

2. List five important characteristics of traditional ecological knowledge.

a) ______________________________

b) ______________________________

c) ______________________________

d) ______________________________

e) ______________________________

3. Traditional ecological knowledge promotes values that are different from Western economic values. These differences are set out in **Figure 1** below.

| Traditional Ecological Values | Western Economic Values |
|---|---|
| • respect for non-human things as individuals | • little respect for non-human things as individuals |
| • recognition and understanding of the bonds and interdependence among humans and non-humans | • little acknowledgement of the relationship between humans and non-humans |
| • appreciation of the importance of local places | • lack of appreciation for local places |
| • recognition of humans as a part of the ecological system | • view that humans are separate from and better than other parts of the ecosystem |
| • recognition of humans' responsibility to care for all elements of their environment | • environment is there for their use |

Figure 1: Differences between Traditional Ecological Values and Western Economic Values

Find a picture of a Canadian landscape (you could use the one on pages 154 and 155 of *Geography Now*) and write two paragraphs, each describing the same landscape in terms of one of these sets of values.

a) Traditional Ecological Description

b) Western Economic Description

# 16.1 Calculating Your Own Ecological Footprint

**How I Am Being Assessed** ______________________________

______________________________________________

1. In order to calculate your own ecological footprint, you need to have certain information. The questions below will help you gather it.

   a) What size is your house or apartment in square metres (length times width in metres times the number of floors, including the basement)? ______________

   b) What is the fuel consumption of your car or your family's car (number of litres per 100 kilometres)? ______________________

   c) What percentage of the food that you eat comes from animals (dairy products as well as meat)? __________________

   d) What percentage of your food is fresh and locally produced? ______________

   e) What percentage of your food is processed, packaged, or imported? __________

   f) What is the population of your city, town, or village? __________________

2. a) To calculate your own ecological footprint, go to the website of the Earth Day Network and click on the heading Your Ecological Footprint. Or you can use the ecological footprint calculators on the Nelson website. To access them, go to www.nelson.com/geographynow, click on Student Centre, then on Web Links, and then on Unit 3.

   b) My ecological footprint is ______________________________________.

   c) Describe your reaction to your personal score.

   ______________________________________________

   ______________________________________________

   ______________________________________________

   ______________________________________________

   ______________________________________________

   ______________________________________________

## 16.2 The Ecological Footprints of Selected Countries

**How I Am Being Assessed** ______________________________

______________________________

1. Convert the information in the bar graph in **Figure 16.6** on page 168 of *Geography Now* into table format, using the two tables below.

| Country | Ecological Footprint in Hectares |
|---|---|
| Bangladesh | |
| Canada | |
| China | |
| India | |
| Mexico | |
| Russia | |
| USA | |
| World Average | |

Table 1: Ecological Footprints of Countries Arranged Alphabetically and World Average Footprint

| Country | Ecological Footprint in Hectares |
|---|---|
| Bangladesh | |
| India | |
| China | |
| Mexico | |
| World Average | |
| Russia | |
| Canada | |
| USA | |

Table 2: Ecological Footprints of Countries by Size of Footprint and World Average Footprint

2. What is the advantage of **Table 1**?

______________________________

______________________________

3. What is the advantage of **Table 2**?

4. What is the advantage of the original bar graph format used in **Figure 16.6**?

5. How could you calculate the number of hectares for each country if the numbers were not printed over the bars in **Figure 16.6**?

6. How many countries in the table are above the world average and how many are below it?

7. How does Canada's ecological footprint compare with the world average?

8. How does Canada's ecological footprint compare with that of the United States?

9. Explain in your own words what it means to be larger or heavier than the world average and what it means to be smaller or lighter than the world average.

10. What are the implications of these statistics for world development in the future?

## 16.3 Becoming an Environmental Steward

**How I Am Being Assessed** ______________________________

______________________________

Read pages 167 to 172 in *Geography Now* and then answer the following questions:

1. What is a steward?

   ______________________________

2. a) What are six ways that you can become an environmental steward?

   - ______________________________
   - ______________________________
   - ______________________________
   - ______________________________
   - ______________________________
   - ______________________________

   b) For each of the above items, give an example of where or how you could do this in your community.

   - ______________________________
   - ______________________________
   - ______________________________
   - ______________________________
   - ______________________________
   - ______________________________

3. Brainstorm solutions to the problems identified in each of the six categories in **Figure 16.10** on page 171 of *Geography Now*. Write three of your ideas for solving each problem on the lines provided in **Figure 1** on the next page.

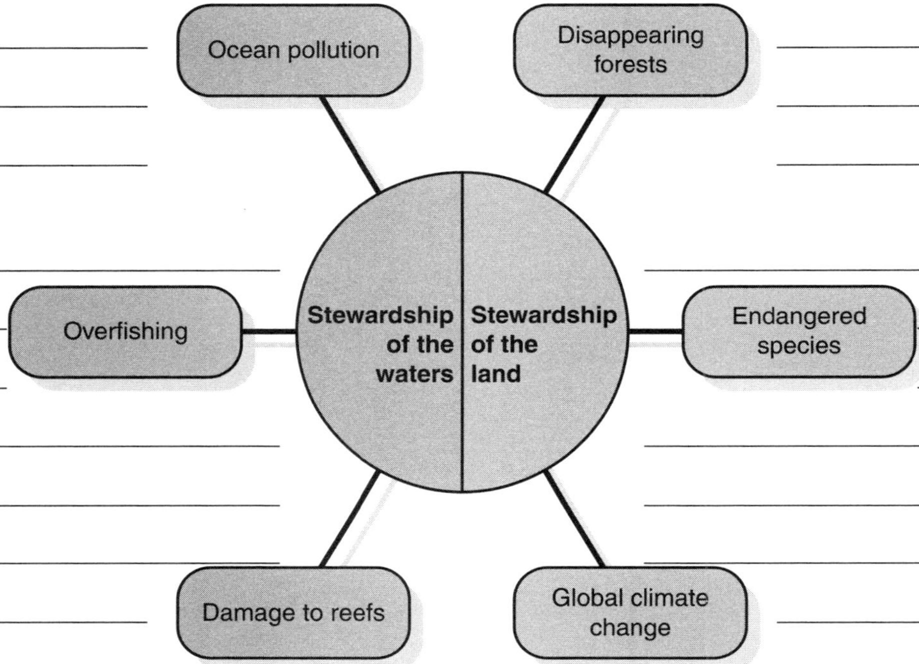


Figure 1: Possible Solutions to Environmental Problems

4. Name five types of stewardship carried out by conservation authorities in Ontario.

i. ______________________________

ii. ______________________________

iii. ______________________________

iv. ______________________________

v. ______________________________

5. a) Why is a career as a soil conservationist a good idea for someone who wants to be a steward of the earth?

______________________________

______________________________

______________________________

______________________________

b) Why is it a good idea to study Geography if you want to have a career as a soil conservationist?

______________________________

______________________________

______________________________

______________________________

______________________________

______________________________

______________________________

______________________________

______________________________

# 17.1 Canada's Energy Sources and Uses

**How I Am Being Assessed** ______________________________

______________________________________________

1. Define and give examples of what is meant by each of the following terms:

   a) renewable energy:

   ______________________________________________

   ______________________________________________

   ______________________________________________

   b) non-renewable energy:

   ______________________________________________

   ______________________________________________

   ______________________________________________

   c) conventional energy sources:

   ______________________________________________

   ______________________________________________

   ______________________________________________

   d) alternative energy sources:

   ______________________________________________

   ______________________________________________

   ______________________________________________

2. **Figure 17.2** on page 175 of *Geography Now* and **Figure 1** on page 100 present the same information about energy use in Canada in 2003. Using the bar in **Figure 2**, present this same information in a horizontal cumulative bar graph. Colour the third column in the table as your legend for the graph. The first block in the graph has been completed for you.

| Type of Use | % | |
|---|---|---|
| Residential uses | 17.3 | |
| Commercial and institutional uses | 13.9 | |
| Industrial uses | 38.4 | |
| Transportation uses | 27.9 | |
| Agricultural uses | 2.5 | |

Figure 1: Table of Total Energy Use in Canada in 2003

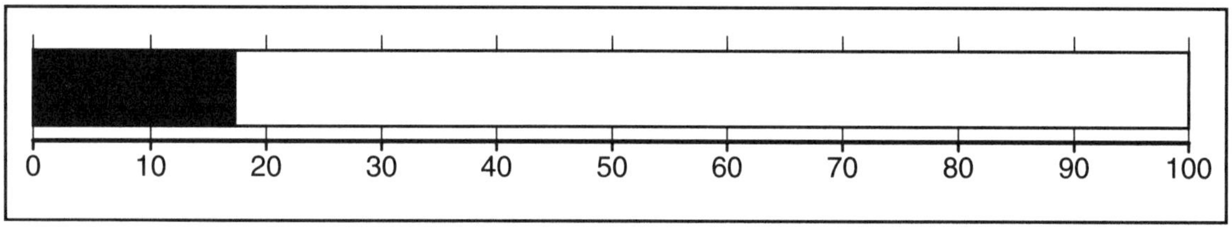


Figure 2: Bar Graph of Total Energy Use in Canada in 2003

3. a) Mark the locations of the following sources of energy on the map of Canada in **Figure 3** on the opposite page:

   i. oil fields  ii. gas fields  iii. coal mines

   iv. uranium mines  v. tar sands

   You can find the information you will need in **Figure 17.3** on page 176 of *Geography Now*.

   b) Supply a title and a legend for your map.

4. Write a paragraph describing the pattern of the locations of these sources of energy in Canada.

_______________________________________________

_______________________________________________

_______________________________________________

_______________________________________________

_______________________________________________

_______________________________________________

_______________________________________________

_______________________________________________

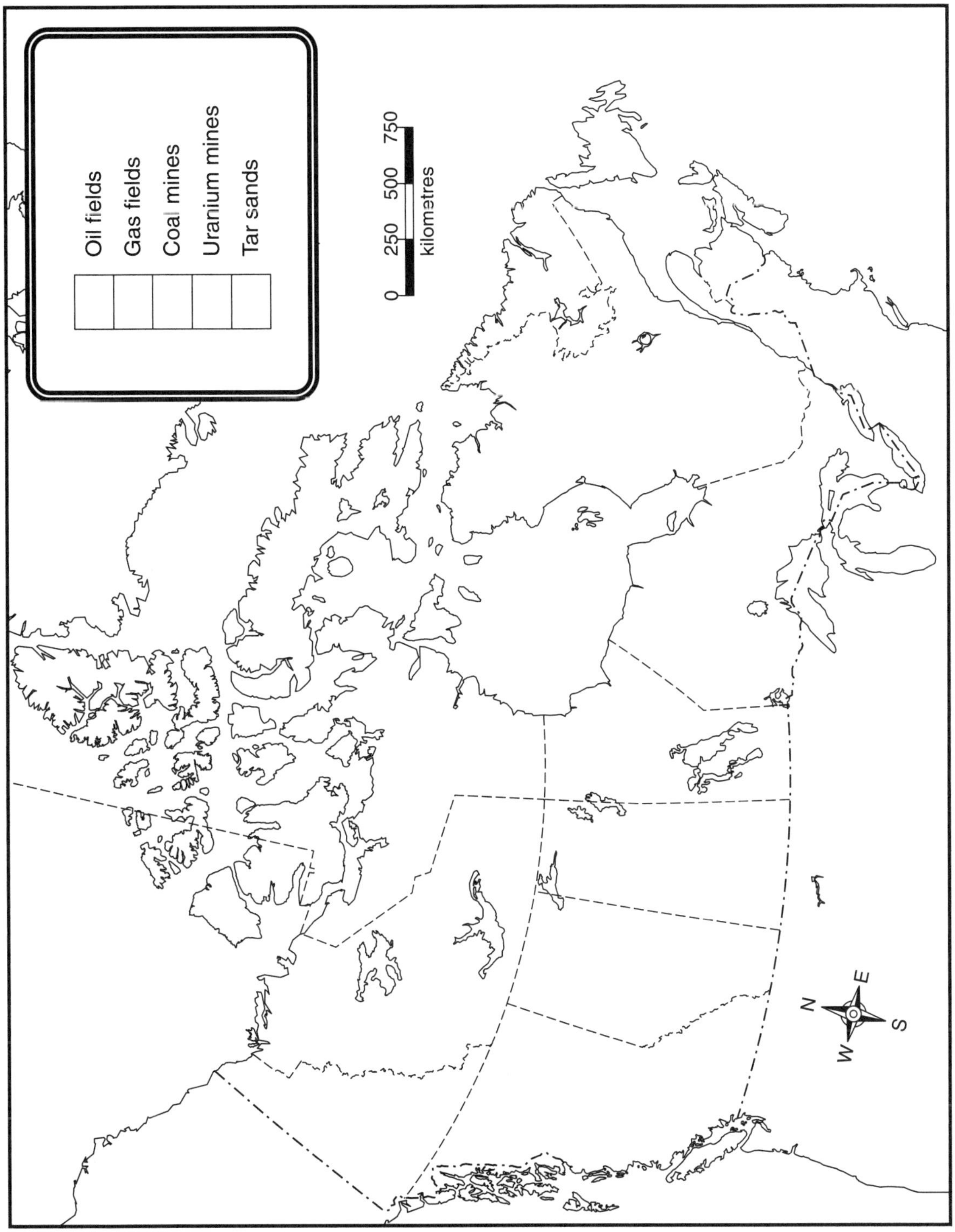
Oil fields
Gas fields
Coal mines
Uranium mines
Tar sands
0
250
500
750
kilometres
N
E
S
W

Figure 3: ____________________

## 17.2 Word Power

**How I Am Being Assessed** ________________________________

________________________________________________

1. Complete the energy crossword puzzle. You will find the solutions to all the clues in Chapter 17 of *Geography Now*.

**ACROSS**

1. Method used to mine the oil sands
7. Type of fossil fuel
9. Type of oil found in the oil sands
12. Many wind turbines in one place
14. Energy from the sun
16. Organic garbage used as a source of energy
17. Energy prices are connected to energy ______.
22. The refined fossil fuel that powers your car
24. Solar, wind, and geothermal are examples of __________ energy sources.
26. Returning the land to its original state after mining is called land _______.
27. Conservation method where we take care not to use up resources so that nothing is left for future generations
28. Bad things about energy sources

**DOWN**

1. Our responsibility to work together to manage natural resources for the benefit of everyone
2. Can be used over and over again
3. Good things about energy sources
4. Energy from inside the earth
5. Hydroelectric power and nuclear power are generated from__________energy sources.
6. Factories where oil is processed
8. Mineral needed to produce nuclear energy
10. A swamp or bog in northern Canada
11. The top layer of earth and debris that covers most of the oil sands
13. ________________ Oil Sands
15. Type of energy found in the Bay of Fundy
18. Are we going to run out of it?
19. Surface mining results in the loss of animal ___.
20. Name of your country
21. Megaproject off the coast of Newfoundland and Labrador
23. Solar ______can heat water.
25. Type of fossil fuel that you cannot use in your car

## 17.3 Alternative Energy Sources

**How I Am Being Assessed** ______________________________

______________________________

1. List three advantages and three disadvantages of various alternative sources of energy in the appropriate columns in **Figure 1** below. Supplement the information you can find in Chapter 17 of *Geography Now* with information obtained from websites.

| Energy Type | Advantages | Disadvantages |
|---|---|---|
| Solar | | |
| Wind | | |
| Tidal | | |
| Biomass | | |
| Geothermal | | |

Figure 1: Advantages and Disadvantages of Alternative Sources of Energy

2. Your local government has decided that it will develop an alternative energy source, **but it can only afford to use one type of alternative energy**. Write a paragraph arguing in favour of one of the energy sources mentioned in question 1. Give at least three reasons why you think it would be the best choice for your community.

3. Design a mascot and a catchy slogan that can be used in a campaign to advertise your alternative energy source in your community. In **Figure 2**, present your mascot and your slogan, which may be serious or humorous.

Figure 2: My Mascot and Slogan for an Alternative Energy Source

## 17.4 Megaprojects

**How I Am Being Assessed** ______________________________

______________________________

Several energy megaprojects have been undertaken in Canada. One of the most controversial was the James Bay Hydroelectric Project. Read the following article about the James Bay Project and then answer the questions about it.

### THE JAMES BAY PROJECT

The James Bay Project is the name of a giant hydroelectric development in northern Quebec. It is a series of dams, dykes, reservoirs, and power stations that have been built to harness the energy of some of the major rivers that drain into James and Hudson bays. The James Bay Project originally had three phases, but only one phase was completed. The size of the original project was gigantic. The rivers drain about 350 000 km$^2$ of Quebec, almost one-fifth of the province. Some of these rivers were diverted and reduced to a trickle; others swelled and flooded their former banks. Eventually, up to 28 000 megawatts of power were to be produced. The area of the reservoirs would equal that of Lake Ontario. The project was launched in 1971 by Robert Bourassa who was then premier of Quebec. Development was planned over several phases.

Phase One of the project was completed in 1985 at a cost of some $16 billion. Five rivers were diverted into La Grande Rivière, almost doubling its flow. The three powerhouses built on La Grand Rivière can generate more than 10 000 megawatts of electric power. They are operated by Hydro-Quebec, the provincially owned electricity-generating company.

Phase Two, or the Great Whale Project, was to consist of power stations on the Great Whale River (Grand Rivière de la Baleine). It would have generated 3212 megawatts of power.

Phase Three would have diverted the Nottaway and Rupert rivers into the Broadback River, where up to eight powerhouses would be built. James Bay is one of the last undeveloped hydroelectric sites in North America. If the whole project had been completed, it would have produced 25% of North America's power.

**Controversy**

The massive James Bay Project has been controversial because of its effect on the environment, and on the Cree Indians who live in northwestern Quebec. The native people had fought the project from the beginning. In 1975, the Cree agreed to let the project proceed for $225 million and control over about 75 000 km$^2$. The Cree launched another legal challenge. The diversion of rivers, the flooding of forests, and the creation of huge reservoirs would have had unknown effects on the environment.

The Cree, along with environmental groups and native-rights supporters, put a great deal of pressure on Quebec to stop the project. In 1992, New York State cancelled an agreement to use Quebec's hydroelectric power. New York did this because of the public outcry against the Great Whale Project and a drop in its energy requirements. The Quebec government was counting on New York's $17.6 billion to help pay for the project.

In November 1994, Jacques Parizeau, who was then premier of Quebec, announced that the Great Whale Project would not go on. If it had been built, the Great Whale Project would have flooded an area almost the size of Prince Edward Island and cost $13 billion.

Source: *Junior Encyclopedia of Canada*
© 2006 Historica Foundation of Canada

1. Summarize the events in the development of the James Bay Project using the following chart.

| Date | Event |
|---|---|
| 1971 | |
| 1975 | |
| 1985 | |
| 1992 | |
| 1994 | |

Figure 1: Chronology of the James Bay Project

2. The James Bay Project was very controversial. There were some good things about it and there were some bad things. Complete the following chart to show what you think the good and the bad things were.

| GOOD Things About the James Bay Power Project | BAD Things About the James Bay Power Project |
|---|---|
| 1. ____________________ | 1. ____________________ |
| 2. ____________________ | 2. ____________________ |
| 3. ____________________ | 3. ____________________ |

## 18.1 Shaded Maps and Population Density

**How I Am Being Assessed** ______________________________

______________________________

1. a) Label each of the municipalities in the Greater Toronto Area (GTA) that are shown in **Figure 1**. You will find the information you need in **Figure 18.5** on page 190 of *Geography Now*.

   b) Colour all the boxes in the right-hand column of the legend in the same colour, but with different depth of shading. The first box should be a very light shade, the next one a darker shade, and the final box the darkest shade.

| **Rate of Growth (%)** | |
|---|---|
| 0.0–7.9 | |
| 8.0–14.9 | |
| 15 and above | |

   c) Use the data from **Figure 18.4** on page 189 of *Geography Now* to shade each municipality with the depth of colour that represents its rate of growth.

   d) Give your map a title and include the legend on the map.

2. a) Which municipality does not fit any of the legend categories on the map?

______________________________

______________________________

   b) Why does it not fit?

______________________________

______________________________

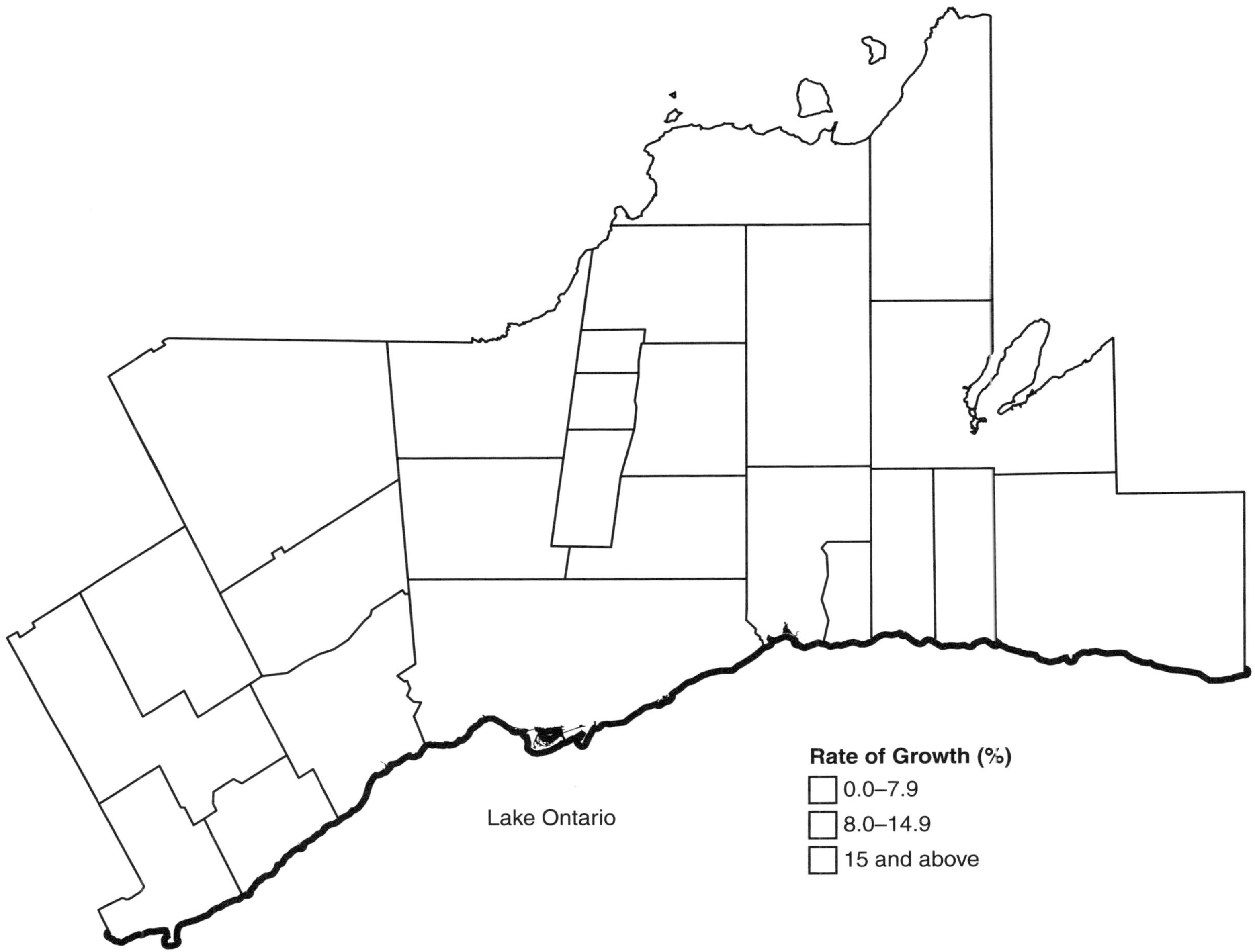


Figure 1: ____________________________

3. Describe the pattern you see in the map in **Figure 1**. Are there concentrations of areas where the population is growing fast or slowly? Try to identify at least three areas in the GTA where you can see some sort of pattern.

4. Differences in population patterns can also be calculated in terms of population density or the number of people per square kilometre (see Chapter 9 of *Geography Now*). Use the information provided in **Figure 2** to calculate the population density of each of the municipalities in the GTA.

   Population density is calculated using the following formula:

$$\frac{\text{Population}}{\text{Area}} = \text{Population Density}$$

   **Example:** Clarington has a population of 69 834 spread over an area of 611.06 $km^2$. Its population density is thus:

$$\frac{69\ 834}{611.06\ \text{km}^2} = 114.3\ \text{people/km}^2$$

   Enter the result in the Density column for Clarington in **Figure 2**. Repeat this calculation to find the population density of all 25 municipalities.

 

| Greater Toronto Area | | | | | | | |
|---|---|---|---|---|---|---|---|
| **Municipality** | **Population 2001** | **Area km²** | **Density** | **Municipality** | **Population 2001** | **Area km²** | **Density** |
| **Clarington** | 69 834 | 611.06 | | **Mississauga** | 612 925 | 288.62 | |
| **Oshawa** | 139 051 | 145.65 | | **Brampton** | 325 428 | 266.43 | |
| **Whitby** | 87 413 | 146.52 | | **Caledon** | 50 595 | 687.04 | |
| **Ajax** | 73 753 | 67.09 | | **Oakville** | 144 738 | 138.51 | |
| **Pickering** | 87 139 | 231.58 | | **Milton** | 31 471 | 366.46 | |
| **Scugog** | 20 173 | 474.62 | | **Halton Hills** | 48 184 | 276.35 | |
| **Uxbridge** | 17 377 | 420.65 | | **Burlington** | 150 836 | 185.71 | |
| **Brock** | 12 110 | 423.73 | | **Toronto** | 2 481 494 | 629.91 | |
| **Markham** | 208 615 | 212.47 | | **East Gwillimbury** | 20 555 | 245.06 | |
| **Whitchurch-Stouffville** | 22 008 | 206.74 | | **Georgina** | 39 263 | 287.72 | |
| **Richmond Hill** | 132 030 | 100.89 | | **King** | 18 533 | 333.04 | |
| **Aurora** | 40 167 | 49.61 | | **Vaughan** | 182 022 | 273.50 | |
| **Newmarket** | 65 788 | 38.07 | | | | | |

Figure 2: Population Density of Municipalities in the Greater Toronto Area

5. Look at the population densities that you calculated and identify at least two different patterns or relationships.

   i. ______________________________

   ______________________________

   ii. ______________________________

   ______________________________

6. a) Which municipality in the GTA has the highest population density?

   ______________________________

   b) What is its population density?

   ______________________________

   c) What municipalities in the GTA have the largest area?

   ______________________________

   d) Which municipality has the lowest population density?

   ______________________________

   e) What is its population density?

   ______________________________

## 18.2 The GTA and the Greenbelt Plan

**How I Am Being Assessed** ______________________________

______________________________

This worksheet is a review exercise. All the answers to these questions can be found in Chapter 18 of *Geography Now*.

Fill in the blanks for the following questions or statements:

1. ______________ and ________________ are types of municipalities.

2. The responsibilities of this level of government affect the whole country.

   ______________________________

3. ______________________________ has put the physical environment in the GTA at risk.

4. In 2001, which municipality had the smallest population? ______________

   How many people lived there? ________ What region is it in? ____________

5. If we exclude the city of Toronto, which region of the GTA had the largest population in 2001? ______________ How many people lived in this region in 2001? ___________

6. For each of the five regions that make up the GTA, identify the municipality that has the highest average earnings:

| | | | |
|---|---|---|---|
| Durham Region | ________________ | average earnings | $ ________ |
| York Region | ________________ | average earnings | $ ________ |
| Peel Region | ________________ | average earnings | $ ________ |
| Halton Region | ________________ | average earnings | $ ________ |
| City of Toronto | ________________ | average earnings | $ ________ |

7. Which municipality lost population between 1996 and 2001? ________________

______________________________________________________________________

8. How much land does the Greenbelt Plan cover? ___________________________

______________________________________________________________________

9. What are environmentally sensitive lands? ______________________________

______________________________________________________________________

______________________________________________________________________

10. Name two major areas that are protected under the Greenbelt Plan.

______________________________________________________________________

______________________________________________________________________

11. The protected countryside is made up of what three areas?

a) ___________________________________________________________________

b) ___________________________________________________________________

c) ___________________________________________________________________

12. What specialty crop is grown on the Niagara Escarpment? ________________

______________________________________________________________________

# 18.3 Greater Toronto Area: Word Search

**How I Am Being Assessed** ______________________________

______________________________

1. Find these words in the puzzle below:

| | | | |
|---|---|---|---|
| COUNTRYSIDE | DEVELOPERS | ENVIRONMENT | ESCARPMENT |
| FARMERS | FEDERAL | GOVERNMENT | GREEN |
| LANDS | MORAINE | MUNICIPAL | NATURAL |
| PARKS | PLAN | POPULATION | PROVINCIAL |
| SETTLEMENT | SPACE | TORONTO | URBANIZATION |

| | | | | | | | | | | | | | | |
|---|---|---|---|---|---|---|---|---|---|---|---|---|---|---|
| M | O | P | B | L | G | O | S | C | T | M | T | S | E | P |
| U | T | E | R | I | A | R | D | N | I | O | S | P | D | O |
| N | S | N | O | O | E | R | E | B | R | D | Z | A | I | P |
| I | G | F | E | M | V | M | E | O | P | A | U | C | S | U |
| C | O | R | R | M | P | I | N | D | P | G | Y | E | Y | L |
| I | A | A | E | R | N | T | N | L | E | Z | B | Z | R | A |
| P | F | Z | A | E | O | O | J | C | B | F | S | L | T | T |
| A | D | C | E | B | N | T | R | B | I | P | Q | A | N | I |
| L | S | N | O | I | T | A | Z | I | N | A | B | R | U | O |
| E | N | A | L | P | A | R | K | S | V | P | L | U | O | N |
| T | N | E | M | E | L | T | T | E | S | N | E | T | C | L |
| D | E | V | E | L | O | P | E | R | S | S | E | A | A | C |
| H | A | E | S | T | M | X | Y | F | F | T | N | N | F | V |
| E | N | I | A | R | O | M | A | S | F | V | D | M | D | S |
| G | O | V | E | R | N | M | E | N | T | S | Y | G | N | R |

## 18.4 Is Everybody Happy? Advocacy Letter

**How I Am Being Assessed** ______________________________

______________________________

As described on page 192 of *Geography Now*, some farmers were not very happy with the Greenbelt Plan. They protested against the plan by driving their farm vehicles along major roads in order to disrupt traffic and get people to understand that they were against this plan.

There are other ways to protest something that you think is unfair. For instance, you could write an advocacy letter to people or organizations that support a decision that you believe is unfair.

Here are a few important points to keep in mind when writing an advocacy letter:

- Try to cover only one subject (in other words, stay on topic).
- Mention the particular plan that you are opposed to by name (in this case, the Greenbelt Plan).
- State specifically why you are opposed to the plan.
- Use facts and data to support your position.
- Keep your letter brief and to the point.
- Avoid slang words.
- Write legibly or type your letter.
- Be original.
- Always sign your name on the letter.
- Be sure to include your full name and address on the letter.
- Be courteous.

1. Pretend that you are a farmer in the Greater Toronto Area, and that you are upset with the government for passing the Greenbelt Plan. Use the space below to brainstorm ideas that you would want to bring to the government's attention.

______________________________

______________________________

______________________________

______________________________

______________________________

______________________________

2. Using the ideas generated in question 1 and following the guidelines for writing an advocacy letter (see opposite page), write a letter that you could send to the government outlining why you are upset about the Greenbelt Plan. Ask the government to reconsider some of the restrictions the plan puts on you and your family. Your teacher will assist you in determining to whom you should address your letter.

# Unit 4 CANADA AND THE WORLD

## 19.1 Website Rating and Evaluation Form

**How I Am Being Assessed** ______________________________

______________________________

1. Find a website that deals with a topic like life expectancy or fair trade. Write down its address here:

______________________________

2. What is the main idea on this website?

______________________________

______________________________

______________________________

3. Write down three facts that are presented on this website.

   a) ______________________________

   ______________________________

   b) ______________________________

   ______________________________

   c) ______________________________

   ______________________________

4. a) Use the AAAA list in **Figure 1** to rate the website by giving it a score of between 1 (poor) and 5 (excellent) for each of the characteristics mentioned in the figure.

   b) Add all your rating points and enter them as the total score.

 

| AAAA: The Four A's for Website Analysis | | | | | |
|---|---|---|---|---|---|
| Score each feature as follows: | Poor | Average | | | Excellent |
| | 1 | 2 | 3 | 4 | 5 |
| **Appeal**<br>Is the site colourful and interesting? | | | | | |
| Are the illustrations clearly titled and explained? | | | | | |
| Are pictures and diagrams linked to the written text? | | | | | |
| Is the content easy to understand? | | | | | |
| **Accuracy**<br>Is the content recent, current, and relevant? | | | | | |
| Is the information free of bias? (See page 193 of *Geography Now* for a discussion on bias.) | | | | | |
| Is the author or the source of the information stated? | | | | | |
| **Appropriate**<br>Does the site contain useful information? | | | | | |
| Is the site suitable for all ages? | | | | | |
| Is the site useful in your research? | | | | | |
| **Accessible**<br>Do the pages load quickly and easily? | | | | | |
| Can you move (navigate) around the site easily? | | | | | |
| Do the links to other sites work properly? | | | | | |
| **Total Score** | | | | | |

Figure 1: AAAA Chart for Website Analysis

5. Write a two-sentence summary giving the total score and your opinion of the site. Explain why this website will or will not be helpful to you or to others.

______________________________________________

______________________________________________

______________________________________________

______________________________________________

______________________________________________

______________________________________________

# 19.2 The Human Development Index

**How I Am Being Assessed** ______________________________

______________________________

1. a) Find and label the ten countries named in **Figure 1** on the world map in **Figure 2**. (You may need to look them up in a world atlas.)

| **Country** | **Area ($km^2$)** | **Population** | **Life Expectancy** (female/male) | **% Primary School Enrolment** (female/male) | **Gross Domestic Product** (per capita) | **Human Development Index** |
|---|---|---|---|---|---|---|
| Brazil | 8 574 215 | 178 470 000 | 73/64 | 97/96 | $7 770 | medium |
| Canada | 9 984 670 | 31 753 000 | 82/77 | 100/100 | $29 480 | high |
| China | 9 596 961 | 1 304 196 000 | 73/69 | 93/92 | $4 580 | medium |
| Democratic Republic of the Congo | 2 344 858 | 52 771 000 | 43/41 | 34/35 | $650 | low |
| Haiti | 27 750 | 8 326 000 | 50/49 | n/a | $1 670 | low |
| India | 3 287 263 | 1 065 462 000 | 65/63 | 76/91 | $2 670 | medium |
| New Zealand | 270 534 | 3 875 000 | 81/76 | 98/99 | $21 740 | high |
| Russia | 17 075 400 | 143 246 000 | 73/61 | 99/99 | $8 230 | medium |
| Switzerland | 41 284 | 7 169 000 | 82/76 | 99/99 | $30 010 | high |
| Thailand | 513 115 | 62 833 000 | 74/65 | 85/87 | $7 010 | medium |

Figure 1: Human Development Index Ratings for Selected Countries

Figure 2: Map Showing Human Development Index Rating for Selected Countries

b) Create a legend box in one corner of the map in **Figure 2**, in which you assign a different colour to each of the three categories of the Human Development Index rating mentioned in the last column in **Figure 1**.

c) Colour each country you identified on the map in the correct colour to match its rating in the Human Development Index.

2. In **Figure 3**, draw three double bar graphs showing the life expectancy of males and females in Canada, Brazil, and the Democratic Republic of the Congo. Remember to label or colour-code the bars to show which bars represent males and which bars represent females. Supply a legend to explain your coding.

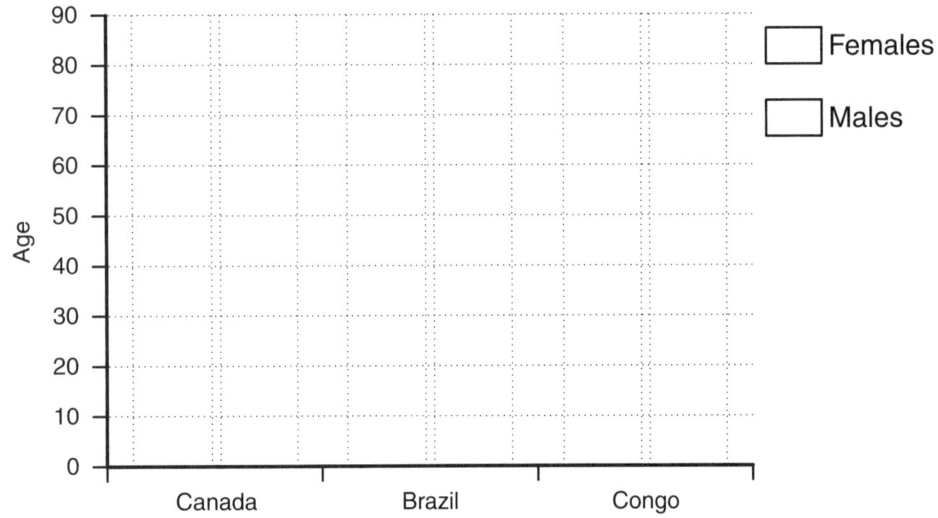


Figure 3: Life Expectancy in Canada, Brazil, and the Democratic Republic of the Congo

3. Write three or four sentences explaining why a high Human Development Index is related to a high Gross Domestic Product and a high percentage of primary school enrolment.

# 20.1 Trade Development in India

**How I Am Being Assessed** ______________________________

______________________________________________________

1. Read the Case Study "Trade in China and India" on page 213 of *Geography Now*. Then answer the following questions:

   a) What are the different paths that India and China are following to earn trade dollars?

   ______________________________________________________

   ______________________________________________________

   ______________________________________________________

   b) Explain why India is specializing in the service sector.

   ______________________________________________________

   ______________________________________________________

   ______________________________________________________

   c) Give two examples of services that produce income for India.

      i. ______________________________________________

      ii. ______________________________________________

   d) Why are the types of services that India is specializing in called information technology (or IT)?

   ______________________________________________________

   ______________________________________________________

   ______________________________________________________

   ______________________________________________________

   ______________________________________________________

2. Read the newspaper article in **Figure 1**. Then answer the questions about it.

TECHNOLOGY

**Dell to double employees in India within three years**

**Dell Inc.** plans to double the number of its employees in India to 20,000 in three years, chairman Michael Dell said yesterday, in what appears to be moves by the world's largest personal computer maker to beef up its presence in one of the world's fastest growing markets. Although most of new hiring will be made at the company's call centres, there will also be substantial recruitment at its product testing centre and a possible manufacturing plant. Dell currently operates four call centres in India, a product testing centre for corporate customers and a global software development centre. Some 10,000 people are employed at these facilities.

Figure 1: Dell Employees in India (*Globe and Mail*, March 21, 2006)

a) Why is Dell choosing to create new jobs in India?

________________________________________

________________________________________

________________________________________

b) What are Dell's plans for its division in India?

________________________________________

________________________________________

________________________________________

________________________________________

c) What work will most of the newly hired employees do for Dell?

d) What operations did Dell run in India in 2005?

e) How will these new service sector jobs offered by an American computer company help India?

## 20.2 Problems in Trade

**How I Am Being Assessed** ________________________________________

________________________________________________________________

1. Read the Case Study, "Trade in China and India" on page 213 of *Geography Now*. Then answer the following questions:

   a) Why is China specializing in making consumer goods for sale?

   ________________________________________________________________

   ________________________________________________________________

   ________________________________________________________________

   b) Give two examples of consumer goods that are produced in China.

   ________________________________________________________________

   ________________________________________________________________

   ________________________________________________________________

2. In 2005, many trade barriers to the importing of textiles and clothing from developing countries were eliminated. The effects of this change on China's trade can be seen in **Figure 1**.

   Note: EU-25 refers to the 25 countries that form the European Union. Q1 2005 refers to the first quarter of 2005 (January to March).

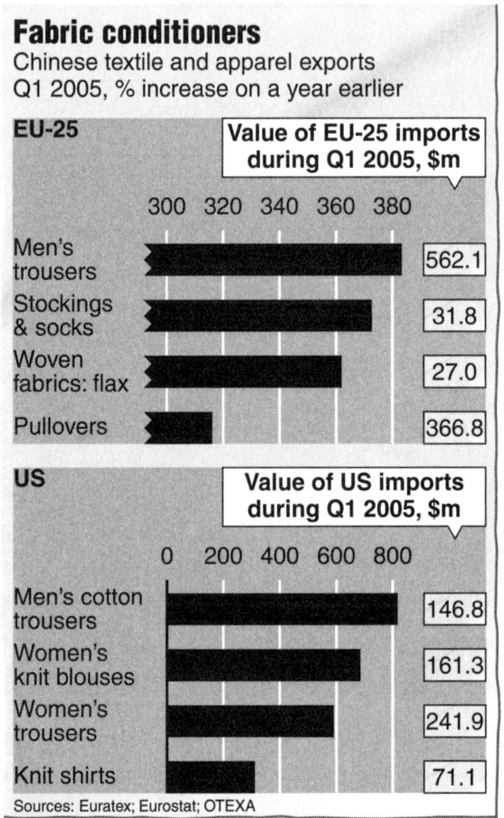


Figure 1: Fabric Conditioners (*The Economist*, June 4, 2005)

a) What do the two bar graphs show?

b) Fill in the columns in **Figure 2**, listing the three leading textile and apparel exports from China to the EU-25 in the first quarter of 2005, the percentage by which trade in each of those items grew in that quarter, and the amount in dollars that those goods earned for China.

| Leading Exports | Growth (%) | Value (US$) |
|---|---|---|
| | | |
| | | |
| | | |

Figure 2: Main Textile and Clothing Exports from China to the EU-25 in 2005

c) Fill in the columns in **Figure 3**, listing the three leading textile and apparel exports from China to the U.S.A. in 2005, the percentage by which trade in each of those items grew in that year, and the amount in dollars that those goods earned for China.

| Leading Exports | Growth (%) | Value (US$) |
|---|---|---|
| | | |
| | | |
| | | |

Figure 3: Main Textile and Clothing Exports from China to the U.S.A. in 2005

d) Why do North American consumers like the trend of importing clothes that are manufactured in China?

e) Why is this trend a problem for the EU-25 and the U.S.A.?

________________________________________

________________________________________

________________________________________

________________________________________

________________________________________

________________________________________

________________________________________

________________________________________

3. Read the following paragraph, and then answer the questions that follow:

Trade issues can cause problems between countries. Over the last decade Canada has had two major trade issues with the United States, its major trading partner. The first of these related to the export of beef. When one Alberta cow was found to have been infected with mad cow disease, the U.S. government put an embargo (ban) on Canadian beef, meaning that it could not be transported across the border for sale in the United States. The embargo ban caused much hardship for Canadian farmers before it was lifted.

The second trade dispute with the United States was about softwood lumber. Canada was accused of dumping its wood products in the United States. "Dumping" is the term used to describe a situation where one country sells goods or services to another at such low prices that the importing country's industries cannot compete. The U.S. government imposed a tariff or duty on Canadian softwood to make it more expensive for U.S. consumers to buy. Because Canadian wood was now more expensive, American consumers bought less of it. The tariff has caused much hardship for Canadian companies that sell wood used in housing and other construction projects in the United States.

 

a) What is an *embargo*?

b) What is a *tariff*?

c) How do embargoes and tariffs like those described in the paragraph opposite affect the following groups in Canada?

i. Companies

ii. Workers

iii. Stores that sell goods in the communities where the affected workers live

iv. Service providers

d) How does this example of how decisions made in another country affect Canadians influence your understanding of the section on "Geography and Quality of Life" on page 204 of *Geography Now*?

 

# 21.1 Impacts of Tourism

**How I Am Being Assessed** ______________________________

______________________________

1. Read the section on the impacts of tourism on pages 224 to 227 of *Geography Now*. Use information from these pages to identify seven benefits of tourism and seven problems caused by tourism. Write your points in the chart in **Figure 1**.

| Benefits of Tourism | Problems Caused by Tourism |
| --- | --- |
| | |

Figure 1: Some Impacts of Tourism

2. Look at the scene in **Figure 21.9** on page 226 of *Geography Now*. In the space opposite, make a sketch to show this scene. Label these items on your sketch:
   - portholes (windows)
   - lifeboats
   - buses
   - parking area
   - ship's communication system
   - mountains in the background
   - name of the ship
   - water
   - benches for sitting

3. Write down three different opinions that you might have about tourism and cruise ships if you were a resident of the community in which the cruise ship in **Figure 21.9** has docked. Explain why you might have each opinion.

| Opinion | Explanation for Opinion |
|---|---|
| | |
| | |
| | |

Figure 3: Opinions About Tourism

4. Think about the community you live in now. List up to five examples of businesses that serve tourists.

_______________________________________________

_______________________________________________

_______________________________________________

_______________________________________________

_______________________________________________

Figure 2: A Cruise Ship in Port

5. a) Identify three problems that tourists have helped to create in the community where you live.

i. ______________________________________________

______________________________________________

______________________________________________

ii. ______________________________________________

______________________________________________

______________________________________________

iii. ______________________________________________

______________________________________________

______________________________________________

b) Identify one action that could be taken to try to solve one problem made worse by tourists.

______________________________________________

______________________________________________

______________________________________________

______________________________________________

______________________________________________

______________________________________________

______________________________________________

______________________________________________

______________________________________________

## How I Am Being Assessed ______________________________

______________________________________________

1. According to **Figure 1**, what are the top three countries visited by tourists from around the world?

______________________________________________

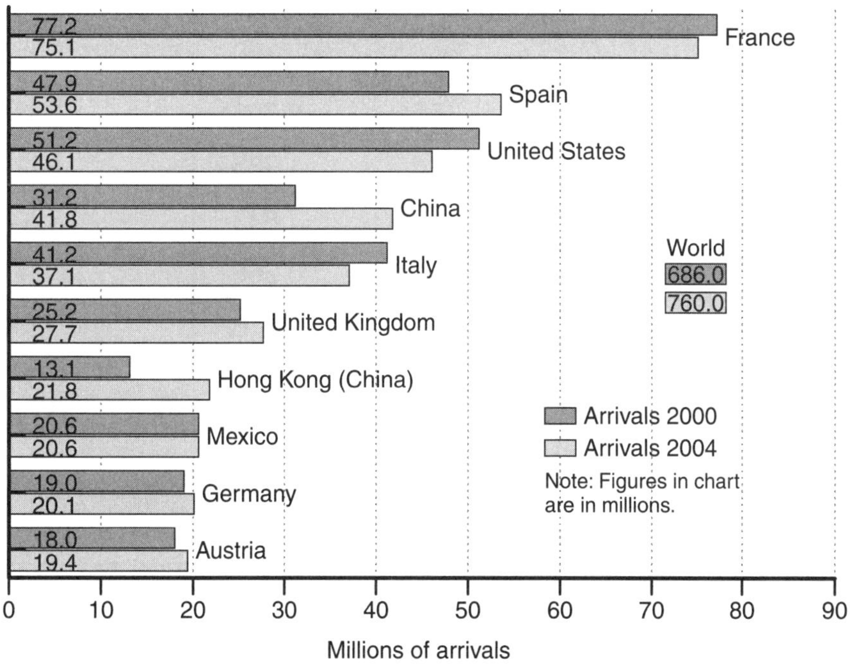


Figure 1: Top Countries for Tourist Arrivals

2. According to **Figure 2** on page 138, what are the top three countries visited by Canadians?

______________________________________________

______________________________________________

______________________________________________

| 2004 Overnight visits | | | |
|---|---|---|---|
| | **Visits** thousands | **Nights** thousands | **Spending in country** C$ millions |
| **Country visited** | | | |
| United States | 13 856 | 107 067 | 8 664 |
| United Kingdom | 754 | 9 718 | 952 |
| Mexico | 705 | 8 023 | 791 |
| France | 590 | 7 592 | 822 |
| Cuba | 570 | 5 204 | 542 |
| Dominican Republic | 527 | 4 729 | 502 |
| Germany | 328 | 3 199 | 270 |
| Italy | 255 | 2 790 | 381 |
| Netherlands | 188 | 1 363 | 121 |
| Spain | 166 | 1 843 | 208 |
| China | 162 | 3 266 | 272 |
| Japan | 161 | 2 076 | 235 |
| Hong Kong | 149 | 2 604 | 212 |
| Ireland | 144 | 1 633 | 185 |
| Switzerland | 142 | 980 | 105 |
| Source: Statistics Canada, Culture, Tourism and the Centre for Education Statistics | | | |

Figure 2: Travel by Canadians to Foreign Countries; Top 15 Countries Visited

3. Where does France rank as a travel choice by Canadians?

______________________________________________

______________________________________________

4. a) Which Canadian province has the strongest cultural ties with France?

______________________________________________

______________________________________________

b) Which province has the second strongest links and why?

______________________________________________

______________________________________________

5. Why do Mexico, Cuba, and the Dominican Republic rank so high on the Canadian list?

6. a) What information does the bar graph in **Figure 1** give you that is not available in the table in **Figure 2**?

b) Why is that information useful?

7. a) What information does the table in **Figure 2** give that is not given in the bar graph in **Figure 1**?

b) Why is this information useful?

8. a) If you could afford to travel, which three places would you like to visit?

b) Write three sentences explaining why you would like to visit your number one choice.

## 22.1 Power to the People

**How I Am Being Assessed** ________________________________________

____________________________________________________________

Read the article in **Figure 1** and then answer the questions about it.

It was only after having many fruitless meetings with firms and policymakers that Mr. Quadir finally hit upon the right approach. He was inspired by Grameen Bank, a Bangladeshi organisation well known for supplying "microcredit", or small loans, mainly to the rural poor. In a typical example, a woman borrows enough money to buy a cow, and then repays the loan using the profits that result from selling its milk. The loan is repaid, the woman earns an income from the cow, and her neighbours can buy milk. Mr. Quadir looked at this model and realised that "a cell phone could be a cow". He formed a consortium with Grameen Bank and Telenor, a Norwegian mobile operator that provided the required telecoms expertise. He was then able to secure loans from development banks and aid agencies, and won a licence from the Bangladeshi government. GrameenPhone launched its service in March 1997, and today has more than 6m subscribers, making it the country's largest telecoms operator. Bangladesh now has six mobile operators and more than 9m subscribers in what has become a booming market.

Around 200,000 of GrameenPhone's subscribers are "telephone ladies" who provide access to telephony in more than 50,000 rural villages, with a total population of 80m people. Despite accounting for a small proportion of the mobile phones in circulation, these "village phones" account for one-third of the traffic on the network, since they are shared between a large number of users. By making telephony widely available, says Mr. Quadir, GrameenPhone has increased the country's GDP by a far greater amount than repeated infusions of foreign aid. Mobile phones promote economic activity, prevent wasted journeys, make it easier to look for work, and widen access to markets. GrameenPhone is not a charity, but a profitable venture: it made net profits of $101m in 2004. Its approach is now being replicated in other countries in Asia and sub-Saharan Africa, including Uganda and Rwanda.

Figure 1: Excerpt from "Power to the People" (*The Economist Technology Quarterly*, March 11, 2006)

1. Where is the country of Bangladesh located?

____________________________________________________________

2. What is microcredit?

____________________________________________________________

____________________________________________________________

____________________________________________________________

3. Describe a typical example of how microcredit works.

4. Which two companies came together to treat a cell phone like a cow?

5. Since 1997, how many subscribers have signed up for the GrameenPhone service?

6. How many mobile (cell) phone operators operate in Bangladesh and how many subscribers do they have?

7. What service do the 200 000 telephone ladies provide?

8. How much of the telephony traffic do these shared village phones provide?

9. How does this system help the economy?

10. Name two other world regions and two other countries that are adopting this kind of phone system.

11. Read the Case Study on page 207 of *Geography Now* and identify one reason why a cell phone system might be better for a developing country than an ordinary phone system.

## 22.2 The Medical Geography of HIV/AIDS in Sub-Saharan Africa

**How I Am Being Assessed** ____________________________________________

______________________________________________________________________

1. a) Mark the locations of the following countries on the map of Africa in **Figure 1**: Angola, Botswana, Cameroon, Ethiopia, Ghana, Lesotho, Mozambique, Namibia, Nigeria, South Africa, Swaziland, Uganda, Tanzania, and Zimbabwe.

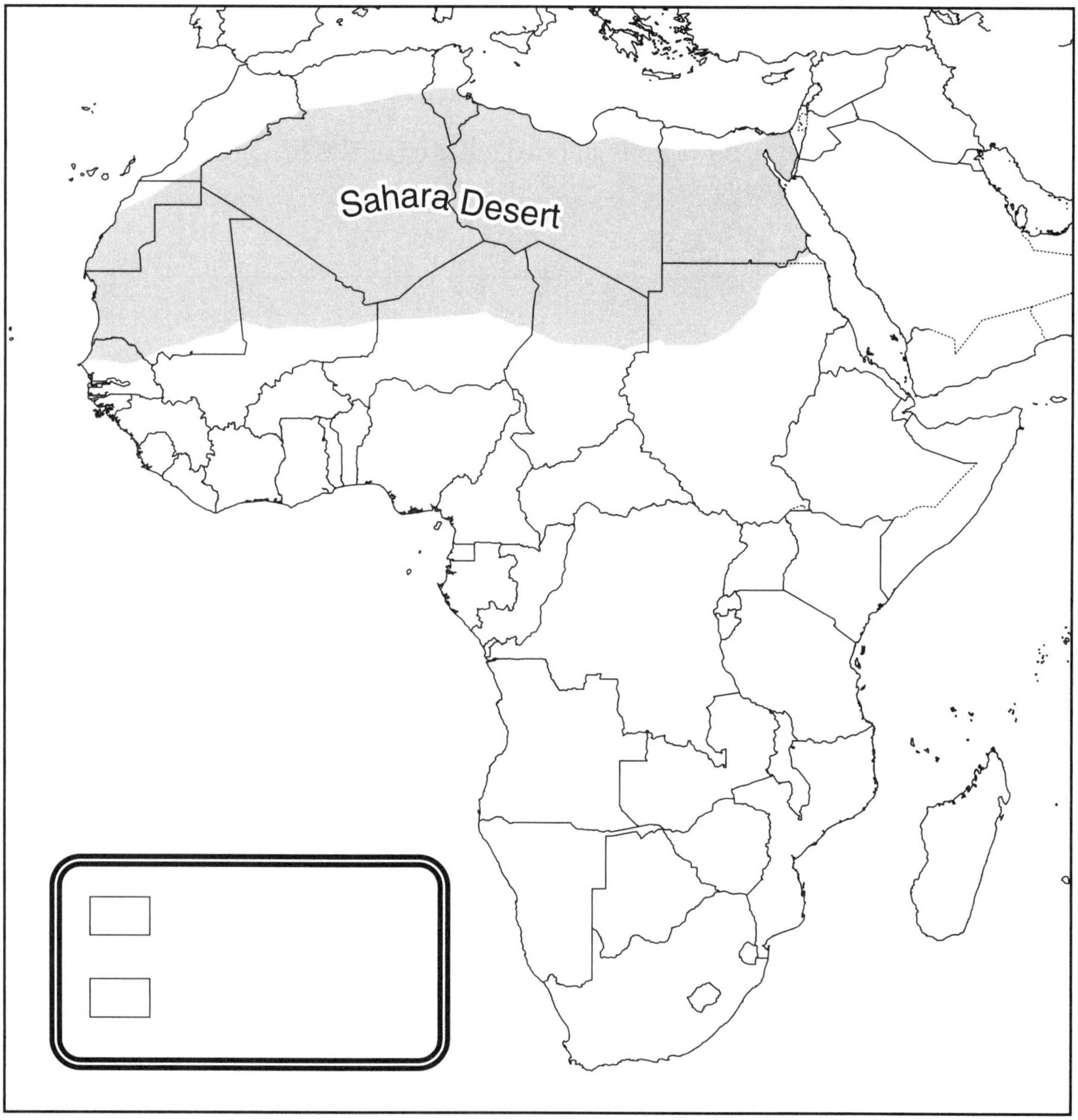


Figure 1: HIV/AIDS in Some Countries in Africa

2. a) What does the term *Sub-Saharan Africa* mean in the heading of **Figure 2**?

b) What direction are they from the Sahara Desert?

| | World | Sub-Saharan Africa |
|---|---|---|
| **Number of people with HIV/AIDS** | 40 million | 26 million |
| **Percent of HIV-positive people aged 15–49** | 1.1% | 8% |
| **Number of children under 18 orphaned by AIDS** | 15 million | 12.3 million |

Figure 2: HIV/AIDS Infections in the World and in Sub-Saharan Africa (adapted from *National Geographic*, September 2005)

c) What percentage of all the people infected with HIV/AIDS live in Sub-Saharan Africa?

3. a) In Botswana, Namibia, Zimbabwe, Lesotho, Swaziland, Mozambique, and South Africa, 10 percent or more of the population has HIV/AIDS. Use colour to identify these countries on the map in **Figure 1**.

b) In Ghana, Nigeria, Cameroon, Ethiopia, Uganda, Tanzania, and Angola, less than 10% of the population has HIV/AIDS. Use a different colour to identify these countries on the map in **Figure 1**.

c) Create a legend for the map.

4. a) Read the following report. Circle or highlight any words that you do not understand and look them up in a dictionary.

HIV/AIDS is a disease that is most often spread through sexual contact. It destroys the immune system that protects the body from diseases. There is no cure, but with expensive drug treatment, AIDS sufferers may live for years, although they will still struggle with side effects from the medication. Mothers may pass the virus on to their babies.

Most people who have HIV/AIDS are young adults. At this stage in their lives, they should be productive workers in society, holding jobs, raising families, and supporting older and younger members of society. But when they have this disease, they are often too ill to work. Their families suffer from poverty. Children are orphaned when their parents die of AIDS.

International aid agencies have focused their activities on educating people about the risk of HIV/AIDS and about how to avoid being infected with the virus (HIV) that causes AIDS.

b) Why is it a particular problem that so many people aged 15 to 49 have HIV/AIDS?

________________________________________

________________________________________

________________________________________

________________________________________

________________________________________

________________________________________

________________________________________

________________________________________

________________________________________

c) If the drugs needed to treat someone infected with HIV/AIDS cost an average of $700 per year, how much money does Africa need each year to treat the 26 million people who are infected with HIV/AIDS?

________________________________________

________________________________________

d) Why is it better to focus on prevention than on treatment for HIV/AIDS?

5. a) Read the Geotechnology box on page 235 of *Geography Now*. How does GIS mapping help people to understand the spread of diseases and take action to control them?

b) How does a GIS map differ from the type of map of Africa you prepared in **Figure 1**?

# 23.1 Looking at Peacekeeping and Peacemaking

**How I Am Being Assessed** ____________________

____________________

1. Read the paragraphs about peacekeeping and peacemaking on page 239 of *Geography Now* and complete this summary page using point-form notes.

**Main Idea**

____________________

____________________

____________________

**First Paragraph Detail**

____________________

____________________

____________________

____________________

____________________

**Second Paragraph Detail**

____________________

____________________

____________________

____________________

**Third Paragraph Detail**

**Conclusion/Connections**

2. **Using the Internet**. Write a brief paragraph on the role Canada has played in peacekeeping in Haiti, the only country in the Americas that has a peacekeeping mission. Your paragraph should mention the role that the RCMP plays in this peacekeeping mission.

# 23.2 Expressing an Opinion on Peacekeeping or Peacemaking

**How I Am Being Assessed** ______________________________

______________________________________________

1. Working with a partner, brainstorm a list of the advantages and disadvantages of Canadians being involved in peacekeeping or peacemaking missions.

______________________________________________

______________________________________________

______________________________________________

______________________________________________

______________________________________________

______________________________________________

______________________________________________

______________________________________________

2. Highlight the three points in your list that you think are most important.

3. Fill in the blanks below to create a draft of a letter you can e-mail to the editor of a newspaper, explaining why you do or do not support Canada's involvement in peacekeeping or peacemaking.

   a) Date: ______________________________

   b) Greeting: ______________________________

   c) Topic Sentence/Statement of Opinion: ______________________

   ______________________________________________

   d) Body Sentences (restate the advantages or disadvantages that you highlighted in your list):

      i. ______________________________

      ______________________________

ii.

iii.

e) Concluding Sentence:

4. Check your draft letter to make sure that all the words are spelled correctly and that the grammar is correct. Make changes as needed.

5. Write a good copy of your letter to the editor here. Be sure to sign your letter.

# 24.1 Facts and Opinions About International Agreements on the Environment

**How I Am Being Assessed** ______________________________

______________________________________________

**Facts** are statements containing information that is known to be true.

**Opinions** are statements that one thinks are true or statements about beliefs based on judgment rather than knowledge.

1. In **Figure 1**, write down three facts and three opinions about yourself.

| Three Facts | Three Opinions |
|---|---|
| | |

Figure 1: Facts and Opinions

2. a) Read the two statements about international environmental agreements on the opposite page. Highlight or underline three facts in each statement.

   b) Reread the two statements, and use a different colour to highlight or circle three opinions.

   ______________________________________________

   ______________________________________________

 

**Statement 1**

Environmental agreements do not help to protect the environment. Just look at all the agreements that Canada has signed and we still have environmental problems. For example, the Great Lakes Charter was signed in 1985, but there is still pollution in the lakes. The tropics contain 50 percent of the world's forests but they are being cut down at a rate of 25 football fields per minute. Just signing pieces of paper does not stop people from doing things that harm the environment.

The biggest problem is that there are too many people on this planet. The world's population is well over 6 billion people and growing quickly. All these people are damaging the environment. There really is no point signing international agreements until the population stops growing.

**Statement 2**

We must do everything that we can to make environmental agreements work. These agreements force individuals, companies, and governments to change the way they do things. For example, the Kyoto Protocol has measures to penalize those countries that do not reduce greenhouse gases. It also encourages average people to reduce greenhouse gases by reducing their energy use by buying better appliances and vehicles. At the present time, Canada produces 2.5 percent of the world's greenhouse gases, a total that is far too high.

The main advantage of international environmental agreements is that they get all of the world's people working toward the same goal — a better physical environment. For that reason alone, we should encourage governments to sign environmental agreements.

3. Some opinions are stated in ways that make them look like facts. Explain why the statement "environmental agreements do not help to protect the environment" is an opinion, even though it may look like a fact.

4. Are facts or opinions more important in an argument? Explain your answer.

5. Write a paragraph explaining why you think international environmental agreements are useful or useless. Your paragraph must include both facts and opinions. (Before you start writing, you may want to look at the Literacy Skill that deals with Organizing Evidence that Supports and Opposes Arguments on page 123 of *Geography Now*.)

## 24.2 Analyzing Internet Sources of Information

**How I Am Being Assessed** ______________________________

______________________________________________

The Kyoto Protocol is an international agreement to reduce greenhouse gas emissions. Some people like this agreement and some people do not. Their opinions are often expressed in pages that they put on the Internet. The pages by the David Suzuki Foundation, the Centre for Research and Information on Canada (CRIC), and the Canadian Manufacturers and Exporters Association are available at www.nelson.com/geographynow.

1. Go to www.nelson.com/geographynow and click on Student Centre, find the page about the Kyoto Protocol from the David Suzuki Foundation, and then complete the following form:

| |
|---|
| **Organization posting website:** |
| **Title of web page:** |
| **First few sentences:** |
| |
| |
| |
| |
| |
| |
| |
| |
| **Main idea:** |
| |
| |
| |
| **Key words that signal the main idea:** |
| |
| |
| |
| |

2. Go to www.nelson.com/geographynow and click on Student Centre, find the page about the Kyoto Protocol posted by the Centre for Research and Information on Canada (CRIC), then fill in the following form:

| **Organization posting website:** |
| --- |
| **Title of web page:** |
| **First few sentences:** |
| |
| |
| |
| |
| |
| |
| |
| |
| **Main idea:** |
| |
| |
| |
| **Key words that signal the main idea:** |
| |
| |
| |
| |

3. Go to www.nelson.com/geographynow and click on Student Centre, find the page about the Kyoto Protocol posted by the Canadian Manufacturers and Exporters Association, then fill in the following form:

| **Organization posting website:** |
| --- |
| **Title of web page:** |

 

| First few sentences: |
| --- |
| |
| |
| |
| |
| |
| |
| |
| |
| **Main idea:** |
| |
| |
| |
| **Key words that signal the main idea:** |
| |
| |
| |
| |

4. Explain why the David Suzuki Foundation might have a completely different view of the Kyoto Protocol than the Canadian Manufacturers and Exporters Association.

5. If you were doing research on the Kyoto Protocol, which of the three websites would give you the most correct information? Explain your answer.

6. When might it be helpful to use a website that does not take a neutral position but argues for or against something?

# PT 4.1 Profile of an International Sporting Event

**How I Am Being Assessed** ______________________________

______________________________________________________

Conduct research and report on a recent international sporting event. Use the Internet or sources in your school's resource centre to find the information that you need to complete this page.

| | |
|---|---|
| Sport:<br><br>Name of Event: | |
| Location: | Dates of Recent Games: |
| Official Logo: | |
| Participating Countries: | |
| Issues or Problems Discussed in the News: | |

## Photo Credits

**7** www.CartoonStock.com;

**24** www.CartoonStock.com;

**69** © Larry Fisher/Masterfile.

## Text Credits

**21-23** Climate data: Canadian Climate Normals or Averages 1971–2000, Environment Canada. Reproduced with the permission of the Minister of Public Works and Government Services Canada, 2006; **36** Source: "Greenpeace shuts down Range Rover assembly line," May 16, 2005, Greenpeace (http://www.greenpeace.org); **126** Source: "Dell to double employees in India within three years," The Associated Press, March 21, 2006. Copyright © 2006 The Associated Press; **128** © 2005 The Economist Newspaper Ltd. All rights reserved. Reprinted with permission. Further reproduction is prohibited. www.economist.com; **138** Source: from the Statistics Canada website <http://www40.statcan.ca/l01/cst01/arts37a.htm>. Extracted April 2006. Statistics Canada information is used with the permission of Statistics Canada. Users are forbidden to copy the data and redisseminate them, in an original or modified form, for commercial purposes, without permission from Statistics Canada. Information on the availability of the wide range of data from Statistics Canada can be obtained from Statistics Canada's Regional Offices, its World Wide Web site at http://www.statcan.ca, and its toll-free access number 1-800-263-1136; **141** © 2006 The Economist Newspaper Ltd. All rights reserved. Reprinted with permission. Further reproduction prohibited. www.economist.com; **144** Map courtesy of Geography at About.com – http://geography.about.com.